STEALING HOME

By
PAT COOK

Dramatic Publishing
Woodstock, Illinois • Australia • New Zealand • South Africa

*** NOTICE ***

IMPORTANT BILLING AND CREDIT REQUIREMENTS

STEALING HOME

CHARACTERS

CECIL . . . . charming conman, around 35

PUG . . . . Cecil's sarcastic sidekick, 30-ish

Officer DOUGHBERG . . . . suspicious 30-year-old cop

BEULAH . . . . kindly and trusting lady, late 60s

JOAN . . . . pretty but wise mortician, late 20s

ZELDA . . . . Beulah's youngest daughter, meek

IMOGENE . . . . Beulah's middle spooky child

GRETCHEN . . . . Beulah's pompous eldest daughter

HUNTER . . . . . well-dressed, long-suffering lawyer, 60-ish

ANGELINA . . . . a nun with a secret

PHOEBE . . . . a no-nonsense psychiatrist

TIME: The present.

PLACE: The lobby of the Green Meadows Funeral Home.

ACT ONE

Scene One

(The setting for our little farce is the large, well-furnished lobby of the Green Meadows Funeral Home. Its walls are covered in wood paneling and support various pastoral pictures and certificates.

There are four entrances to the area. The first, or front door, is located R. The second are double doors, which are located center on the upstage wall. Just L of the double doors on the upstage wall is the third door which leads to the manager's office. The fourth door is located on the R wall and leads to storage.

The furniture in the room, like the walls, is old-fashioned but comfortable. A large sofa rests DL, facing out. There is a matching high-back chair on its upstage arm at a right angle to the sofa. A dark wood coffee table sits in front of the sofa. Near the R door is a heavy desk and chair. Another occasional chair sits in front of it. There is a computer and monitor on top of the desk alongside a telephone. There are double windows on the R wall, downstage from the desk. Also tufted chairs flank the double doors.

AS THE LIGHTS COME UP, there is no one in the room. After a brief pause, the L door creaks open and PUG looks out. He looks around and then tiptoes into the room. Checking the room again, he pulls out a cell phone.)

PUG *(into his phone).* Hey, Cecil! It's me, Pug. *(A brief pause.)* How'd you know it was me? I can't help it I sound like that; I had my tonsils out the same time my voice changed. For two years after that every time I said something people thought it was foggy out. I'm in. No, I gave up on that one but got in the place next to it. Listen, this place is really plush, easy pickin's. Hang on, let me finish casing the joint. *(He moves to the upstage double doors. Carefully, he opens one and eases out, closing the door after him.)*

(After another brief moment, the R door handle jiggles. Then the door gently opens and CECIL enters. He is holding a cell phone as he looks around. He puts the cell phone to his ear.)

CECIL. Pug! *(Brief pause, then disgustedly.)* Who were you just talking to, it's Cecil. You have the attention span of a gnat. Listen, forget your place, I just jimmied open the door of some establishment or other. No, the front door. Let me check to see if the coast is clear. *(He looks around and spies the L door and tiptoes over to it. He easily opens is and exits.)*

(PUG enters through the double doors.)

PUG. What kinda place is this? Large hall with lots of long benches. *(His eyes widen.)* Oh, jeez, I hope I ain't broke into no church! I better check. *(He moves to the front door and exits.)*

(At that moment, CECIL re-enters through the L door.)

CECIL. I can't believe somebody left that window open in here. *(He takes out his cell phone again and pushes a button. Putting it to his ear he speaks.)* Pug! Where are you? What do you mean you're in some church! This ain't no time for that! Get over here! No, the place next to the one we was casing, pay attention! *(He turns off the phone and moves to the double doors. He exits.)*

(At that moment, PUG rushes through the front door.)

PUG *(out of breath)*. Jeez, that was close! That's all we need is to have a cop car in the neighborhood. *(He catches his breath and moves to the desk.)* Maybe I can find out something about this place. *(He thumbs through some papers. Then he hears a noise.)* Oh, jeez! *(He quickly ducks behind the desk. He looks around the downstage end of the desk but doesn't look up or over it.)*

(CECIL enters through the double doors and looks around. He scratches his chin as he thinks. At that moment, PUG pulls out his cell phone. Clumsily, he drops the phone, causing CECIL to look around anxiously. He quickly ducks behind the sofa. He moves to the

downstage end of the couch and listens. PUG listens a moment but doesn't hear anything. He then pushes a button on his cell phone. CECIL's cell phone rings. Quickly CECIL slams a hand over is pocket muffling the ring. Hearing this, PUG looks up over the desk. CECIL pulls out his phone and whispers into it.)

CECIL. What IS it?!

(Hearing this, PUG ducks down behind the desk and answers his phone.)

PUG *(whispering)*. Cecil! It's me!

(Hearing this CECIL speaks into his phone.)

CECIL. Hang on! *(He looks up over the sofa. He then shrugs, ducks down and whispers again into his phone.)* What?!

(On hearing this PUG looks up over the desk again. He shrugs and ducks down.)

PUG. Thought somebody came in here for a minute.
CECIL. Wow, you're kidding! Me, too.

(Both men stop as if hearing something. First PUG rises, looks quickly and ducks down again. Then CECIL rises, quickly looks around and, like PUG, ducks behind the couch. The two whisper back and forth.)

PUG. Man, this place is really plush!

CECIL. Where ARE you?

PUG. Not sure.

CECIL. Describe it.

PUG. Large lobby, lots of wood paneling. Right now I'm behind this large desk.

CECIL. What?

PUG. I said a large desk. There's also a heavy sofa.

CECIL *(after a slight pause)*. Heavy sofa? AND a large desk? *(It's dawning on him.)* Tell me, Pug, is there a chair next to the couch?

PUG. Hang on. *(He pops up, nods as he sees the chair and ducks down again.)* Yeah.

CECIL. And in the room are there double doors? On your left? *(PUG pops up and looks to his right.)* Your OTHER left.

PUG *(seeing the double doors)*. Right!

CECIL. No, your LEFT!

(On hearing this, PUG drops down again.)

PUG. Cecil!

CECIL *(disgustedly)*. Yessss?

PUG. These cell phones you got us are great! It sounds just like you're in the same room with me.

CECIL. Now, Pug, listen to me VERY carefully. *(A beat.)* Are you listening?

PUG *(screwed up expression)*. Just as hard as I can, Cecil.

CECIL *(slowly as if talking to a child)*. Good. Now, what I want you to do is stand up from behind the desk.

PUG. My desk?

CECIL *(long pause)*. How many desks you got? Just STAND UP!

(Together PUG and CECIL rise slowly from their hiding places.)

PUG *(points to CECIL)*. How'd you DO that?

CECIL. Get over here! *(He moves to the center of the room.)*

PUG *(moves to CECIL)*. Wow, one minute I'm casing a joint and you're casing another joint and then… *(He thinks.)*

CECIL *(to himself)*. And as he stumbles into the clearing a light begins to dawn.

PUG. But maybe I wasn't in a different place and neither was you. *(He points at CECIL.)*

CECIL. Yes?

PUG. We're someplace else!

CECIL. As opposed to here?

PUG *(thinks)*. Wait—

CECIL *(puts an arm around PUG)*. Pug, do you know why we write "Pug" on all your clothes?

PUG. Why?

CECIL. 'Cause neither one of us can spell "Ignoramus." *(He shoves PUG to one side.)* Let's get out of here. *(He moves to the front door.)*

PUG. No, no, bad idea.

CECIL *(stops)*. Oh, look who's the idea man. *(He turns to PUG.)* Question. Who's the head of this outfit?

PUG. Now you know we never figured that out. Every time we voted it always come up a tie.

CECIL *(mournfully)*. I know—all sixteen times.

PUG. Anyways, what I was trying to tell you is I was just outside and seen a cop car cruising the neighborhood.

CECIL. Oh. Good call.

PUG *(proudly)*. Yeah. For somebody what can't spell "Ignoramamusmouse."

CECIL *(looks around)*. Okay, drop it.

PUG *(finishing his thought)*. "micemus." *(CECIL glares at him.)* Cheese Whiz!

CECIL *(laughs loudly)*. Oh, stop it. You know that always cracks me up.

PUG. I know. Whenever you is in a foul mood all I have to do is say "Cheese Whiz."

CECIL *(controls himself)*. Yeah, yeah.

PUG. You figure out what this place is yet?

CECIL. No, I was too busy playing "Dial M for Moron." *(He moves to the desk.)* Anything here?

PUG. I was just looking there when I heard a noise. So it's your fault.

CECIL. What's my fault?

PUG. Dunno. I just figured whenever you ask me a question I try to blame it on you.

CECIL. Yeah. *(He picks up a large, hard-backed folder.)* What was I thinking?

PUG. It works.

(CECIL shoots PUG a look and then reads the front of the folder.)

CECIL *(reading)*. "Green Meadows Funeral Home." *(He shrugs and looks at PUG.)* Oh, that explains it. The reason— *(It suddenly sinks in and he drops the folder on the desk.)* Funeral Home?!

PUG. DoWHAT?!

CECIL. Funeral home, it says funeral home!

PUG. You mean this place…this is one of those…this is where they take in… *(He hugs CECIL gently.)*

CECIL. Man, if this just isn't our luck? Of all the places to crack we bust into a morgue!

PUG. No wonder it's so quiet in here.

CECIL. Yeah, I was wondering… *(He looks at PUG.)* I'm not crowding you, am I? *(PUG looks at him.)* You wanna let GO of me?

PUG *(reluctantly breaks the hug)*. Sorry, but these places give me the creeps.

CECIL. They're not designed to give you the "warm fuzzies." *(He looks around.)* I know what you mean about the place being quiet, though.

PUG. I wondered why we didn't set off no alarms when we come in.

CECIL. Makes sense. I mean, you'd have to be really stupid to break into a funeral home. *(He and PUG both laugh and then CECIL stops suddenly.)* That's not funny. *(PUG keeps laughing as CECIL glares at him. PUG winds down his laugh. He picks up the folder again.)*

PUG. Hee hee. *(CECIL shoots him a look.)* Had a couple of leftovers. So what do you think? We ought to blow?

CECIL *(looking through the folder)*. Probably should.

PUG. No point in looking around anymore, right? *(CECIL moves to the sofa, turning the pages of the folder.)* I mean, nothing more for us here. After all, we can't rob a funeral home…can we?

CECIL *(looks at PUG)*. Pug!

PUG. Well? They can't take it with them; maybe they left it here.

CECIL *(sits on the sofa)*. Sometimes you are an embarrassment, you know that?

PUG *(moves to CECIL)*. Well, you always say it doesn't hurt to ask questions. *(He sits.)*

CECIL. Yeah, yeah. *(He turns the page.)*

PUG. You're always asking ME things?!

CECIL. Yeah but those are usually along the lines of "Where did you get that dog?" and "Are you going to stay in there all day?!" *(He turns another page.)* Will you LOOK at all this stuff?

PUG. What? That ain't one of them instruction books, is it? You know, *Grave Digging for Dummies*, that kind of thing?

CECIL. Look at all the stuff you get when you croak! Coffins, flowers, people to speak at the funeral—

PUG *(looking over CECIL's shoulder)*. Really? They sure make it sound great.

CECIL *(without looking up)*. Makes you hot to go, huh?

PUG. Well, I wouldn't say that.

CECIL *(indicating the folder)*. Page after page. Grave markers, tombstones— *(He corrects himself.)* Excuse me, monuments.

PUG. No kidding. Hey, remember when Thumbs Malloy croaked and we went to his send-off?

CECIL. Uh huh. I never saw so many pairs of sunglasses in my life.

PUG. And those funeral people put all his aliases on his tombstone?

CECIL. Yeah, that thing musta been nine feet high. *(He turns a page.)*

PUG. Uh huh, birds kept running into it.

CECIL. Oh, get this. If you buy this plan early you get twenty percent off.

PUG. The price or the coffin?

CECIL. They're not going to bury you in some box without the lid. Here, see? You receive a copper casket,
complete with cedar lining, linen pillows and a tux!

PUG. Wow!

*(Unseen by the two burglars, Officer DOUGHBERG en-
ters quietly through the front door. He looks around and
sees the boys.)*

CECIL. You'd look better than you EVER did.

PUG. Yeah, and nobody there would recognize me.

CECIL. And you get mourners, pall bearers, an eternal
flame—

PUG. Does that mean it never goes out?

(DOUGHBERG nods and moves to the burglars.)

CECIL. Of course, that's what eternal means. And the price
is negotiable should the deceased prove a hardship case.
(He looks up.) Isn't that a plus. *(He sees DOUGHBERG
who nods to him, grinning. Without missing a beat
CECIL continues, now in a mournful voice.)* So you see,
Mr. Hoskins, we can offer you a wide range of services,
depending on your needs.

PUG. Huh?

CECIL. Our establishment works with the family to make
sure all your funeral needs are not only met but satisfac-
torily so.

PUG. But— *(He sees DOUGHBERG and quickly turns
back to CECIL.)* What about songs, can I choose my favorite song?

CECIL. We fulfill all your wishes to the letter. And should you die suddenly—

PUG. Why, have you heard something?

DOUGHBERG. Okay, you two, on your feet.

CECIL. Why, Officer, I didn't see you there. *(Looks at PUG.)* Mr. Hoskins, you see how well our establishment is protected.

PUG. Yea verily. *(He looks at DOUGHBERG.)* A gracious good evening to you, sir.

CECIL. And what, may I be so bold as to inquire, brings you to our firm on such a night?

DOUGHBERG. Just doing my job. Now up. *(He motions them to rise.)*

PUG. But I haven't picked my tunes yet.

CECIL. You have a favorite song?

PUG. Well, I used to like "Let the Lower Fires Be Burning," but under the circumstances—

DOUGHBERG. UP, I said.

(CECIL and PUG slowly rise.)

CECIL. Is something amiss, Officer?

DOUGHBERG. You might say that.

CECIL. May I have your name?

PUG. Now, that's silly. What's HE going to use?

DOUGHBERG. Oh, they all know me around here. Name's Officer Doughberg.

CECIL. Doughberg?

(PUG hears this and giggles.)

DOUGHBERG. What's so funny?

PUG. Doughberg!

CECIL *(aside to PUG)*. Nix, Pug, not a good time.

PUG. But Doughberg? *(He giggles again.)*

DOUGHBERG *(getting irritated)*. It's an old family name!

PUG. Can't you just see it? Some ship is sailing up north and then they suddenly see this huge biscuit! *(He pulls on CECIL's sleeve, trying to control himself.)*

DOUGHBERG. Okay, okay, fun's over. You know who I am so who, may I be so bold to inquire, are you?

CECIL. Me? Well, I'm…I'm… *(He glances at the folder.)* …yes, like it says right here, I am your after-life counselor.

DOUGHBERG. Oh really? *(He looks at CECIL's clothes.)* This is how you dress when doing business?

CECIL *(looking down as his clothes)*. Uh—Casual Friday?

PUG. That's one of the reasons I like this place, very friendly. I come here all the time.

DOUGHBERG. You DO?

CECIL. Uh…he has a large family.

PUG. Well, HAD a large family.

CECIL *(moves to DOUGHBERG)*. Now, what about you, sir?

DOUGHBERG. Me? What ABOUT me?

CECIL. Well, have you made plans for your departure?

DOUGHBERG *(surprised)*. Huh?

PUG. Shouldn't wait until the last minute, you know.

CECIL. Yes, remember it's only sixty seconds.

DOUGHBERG *(thinking)*. Well, I never thought of that.

CECIL. Now is the time to make your move. After all, it'll be your last relocation.

PUG. And they can give you twenty percent off if you act now. They'll even throw in the lid.

DOUGHBERG. Well, I always figured the force would provide for me. And even then— *(He catches himself.)* HOLD IT! Stop stalling, you two. Let's see some identification and I mean right now!

CECIL *(pats his jacket)*. Ah, yes. Credentials, credentials, now WHERE did I leave my wallet?

DOUGHBERG *(to PUG)*. What about you? You got anything with your picture on it?

PUG. My picture? Shoot, the last time somebody wanted my picture they asked for my fingerprints too.

(CECIL elbows PUG.)

DOUGHBERG. That's what I thought. *(With both hands, he grabs CECIL and PUG by their arms.)* Let's go. Into the squad car with the both of you! *(DOUGHBERG ushers CECIL and PUG to the front door.)*

CECIL. See here, Officer, there has been some misunderstanding.

PUG. You can't do this!

DOUGHBERG. Oh no? *(He taps his badge.)* See this badge? It says I can take in any suspicious characters. And, brother, do YOU guys fit the bill!

(At the moment, BEULAH enters through the manager's door. She sees the others.)

CECIL. I don't believe that calls for this sort of roughhouse. After all, you can't judge a book by its cover.

DOUGHBERG. No, but I can throw the book at YOU!

PUG. Ooh, well played.

BEULAH *(eyes widen)*. Oh my! I don't believe it. But... it's HIM!

DOUGHBERG. Do I have to use force?

CECIL. Now, now, let's be reasonable. If I could just show you my credentials. *(He snaps his fingers.)* I know—I bet I left them in my office. *(He starts to move.)* If I may go and look—

DOUGHBERG. Oh NO you don't! *(He grabs CECIL.)*

BEULAH. After all these years, he DID come home!

DOUGHBERG. Don't think you can pull that old one on me, I don't have time—

BEULAH *(hand up)*. Officer Doughberg?

DOUGHBERG. Hah? *(He turns and sees BEULAH. He immediately lets go of CECIL and takes off his cap.)* Mrs. Meadows!

CECIL. Huh?

(CECIL and PUG turn and see BEULAH.)

PUG. Now we're in for it.

(BEULAH moves to the others.)

BEULAH. Thank you, Officer, thank you SO much!

DOUGHBERG. Just doing my duty, is all, ma'am.

BEULAH. Where did you FIND him?

DOUGHBERG. Right here, Mrs. Meadows, and don't worry, I have things well in hand.

BEULAH. After all these years! *(She hugs CECIL.)* You've come home!

CECIL. Of course, I—dowhat?

BEULAH. After twenty-five years, I KNEW you'd finally regain your memory in time.

PUG *(to CECIL)*. What did you do? *(CECIL shrugs.)*

DOUGHBERG. What ARE you talking about, ma'am?

BEULAH *(indicates CECIL)*. Him! My darling Jimmy! He's come home! Home at last, my long lost son, Jimmy!! *(She hugs him again.)*

DOUGHBERG, CECIL & PUG. WHAT?

(LIGHTS black out.)

Scene Two

(It is an hour later. CECIL and PUG are now seated on the couch. In front of them on the coffee table is a tray of sandwiches. The two are greedily munching on the food. The L door is open.)

PUG. This is really good. Wha'd you get?

CECIL. Tuna salad. You?

PUG. Pastrami. And the good kind, too, doesn't have those berries in it.

CECIL. That's pepper loaf you're thinking about. *(He looks behind himself at the L door.)*

PUG *(he leans in to CECIL)*. Hey, how you figger that old dame getting us off the hook like that?

CECIL. I don't know, but it's a sure bet she's got something up her sleeve. People just don't do something for nothing. And if we hang around I'm sure she'll tell us so let's just eat up and beat it.

PUG. Good plan. *(He munches on his sandwich.)*

(BEULAH enters through the L door carrying a tray on which is a pitcher of tea and two glasses with ice in them.)

BEULAH. I'm sorry I don't have your favorite, Jimmy. I knew something was going to happen tonight, I just knew it. *(She places the tray on the coffee table.)* I could feel it in these old bones of mine.

CECIL. Well, it sure surprised us.

BEULAH. There's something for you to drink.

CECIL. Thank you. *(He pours the tea into the glasses.)* We really appreciate you standing up for us, ma'am.

PUG. You can say that again.

CECIL. But we were just wondering what it is we can do for you?

BEULAH. Do for me? *(She leans over and runs her hand through CECIL's hair to straighten it.)* You already have, Jimmy. You came home.

CECIL. I did?

BEULAH. All those years I waited. I just knew you'd finally get your memory back. And tonight, I don't know, I just had a feeling…

CECIL. I'm Jimmy? You think I'm—

BEULAH. I know you probably don't remember how it all happened.

CECIL. Uh…well, why don't you tell my friend here? I'm sure he'd like to hear it.

PUG *(elbows CECIL)*. Why don't YOU tell me? *(CECIL elbows him back.)*

CECIL *(through clenched teeth)*. I can't remember, RE-MEMBER?! *(BEULAH looks at PUG. CECIL sees this.)* Oh where are MY manners? This is my friend—

PUG *(hand out)*. Parnell Debussy Hoskins.

(BEULAH gratefully shakes PUG's hand as CECIL stares at him in disbelief.)

CECIL *(coming to)*. Anyway, you were going to tell…him! *(He shoots PUG another dirty look.)*

BEULAH. All those years ago and still it seems like yesterday. I blame myself, you must know that. You see we had gone to that amusement park. *(To CECIL.)* You were only seven at the time. *(To PUG.)* And he just HAD to ride that roller coaster. That's all he talked about all the way to that place, that horrible roller coaster. He was SO happy when he got on. Then after the ride took off something happened, we never found out exactly what, but he fell out of his car!

PUG. Oh, my!

BEULAH. And apparently he hit his head, something like that, because he was unconscious when we got to him. They had this first aid station there so we rushed him over there. He was put on a cot and finally came to. Well, that was a blessing. But then we noticed he was acting odd, saying strange things, asking us all sort of questions. He…he didn't recognize any of us. Even me, his own mother.

PUG *(sympathetically)*. Aw, that's so sad.

BEULAH *(looks at CECIL)*. Yes. But then, when we stepped outside to talk to the doctor he told us that you'd probably come out of it. But of course we never had the chance to find out.

CECIL. How come?

BEULAH. Because when we went back to be with you you were gone! We looked and looked for you! Even after the park closed. We called in the police and they searched. But we never found you. *(She leans over and kisses CECIL on his forehead.)* But that's all behind us now. And I promise that I will make it all up to you.

(CECIL stares at her, wide-eyed. PUG sips his tea and makes a face.)

PUG. Ugh? You have any sugar, ma'am?

BEULAH. Oh, where is my mind? I guess I'm still a bit giddy. *(She moves to the L door.)* I'll get you some right away. *(She exits.)*

CECIL *(accusingly, to PUG)*. Parnell Debussy Hoskins?!

PUG. That's my real name. What, you think when I was born they named me "Pug"?!

CECIL. She ain't running any scam! She REALLY thinks I'm her son.

PUG *(leans in to CECIL)*. You SURE you're not holding out on me?

CECIL. Will you stop it?!

(PUG gets up. CECIL looks at the L door again.)

PUG. Okay, now's our chance.

CECIL. Huh?

PUG. Let's us leave.

CECIL. Oh, right. *(He rises.)*

PUG *(moves to the front door)*. Just hope little boy blue ain't still out there.

CECIL. Ooh, good point. Take a gander.

(PUG gently opens the front door and peeks out. CECIL again looks at the L door.)

PUG. I don't see nothing. *(He turns to CECIL.)* You ready? *(He gets no reply from CECIL.)* Cecil!

CECIL. Huh?

PUG. You ready? *(He indicates the door.)*

CECIL. Hang on a minute. Maybe we're missing a bet here.

PUG. How you figger?

CECIL. Why not just let this one ride?

PUG. Dowhat? *(He closes the door and moves to CECIL.)*

CECIL. I mean, the old dame figgers me to be this lost boy of hers, this Jimmy, what-say we go with that?

PUG. You mean we stick and you keep acting like him?

CECIL. Sure.

PUG. How can you act like somebody nobody has seen for umpteen years?

CECIL. That's the beauty of it, Pug.

PUG *(looks at him quizzically)*. How? I mean how can you keep on being somebody you ain't?

CECIL. Just my point, doofus. How can anyone prove I'm NOT him? *(He leans in to PUG.)* No matter what they can dig up on me, my real past, how can anybody prove it didn't all begin AFTER I ran away and lost my memory?

PUG. Wow. Say, that IS a great plan. *(He looks around the room.)*

CECIL. I mean, we didn't think this one up, right? And, after all, we'll be making the old lady happy, see?

PUG. Yeah. *(He likes the idea.)* YEAH. *(Again he looks around.)*

CECIL. What? What're you looking around for?

PUG. Oh, I was just thinking. It'd be nice to have a home. You know, a REAL home; not just living out of our car from town to town.

CECIL. That would be sweet, wouldn't it? *(He, too, looks around.)*

PUG. Hot meals, clean sheets on a warm bed. *(Excitedly.)* And then maybe I can finally get a dog!

CECIL. Here you go again, you and dogs.

PUG. That's what I was just thinking. *(He looks around again.)* Being here just put me in mind of it. *(CECIL looks at him curiously.)* Well, I always figgered that when it's my time to go, you know, leave this earth, I don't know where I'll end up but if there be dogs there it'll be heaven enough for me.

CECIL *(hand on PUG's shoulder)*. Why, Pug, that's a lovely thought.

(PUG bows his head in embarrassment. Then he scowls and looks up at CECIL.)

PUG. What, you don't think I can have ideas like that?

CECIL. Oh, never mind! *(He looks over at the L door.)* Quiet, here she comes!

(The two quickly sit on the sofa again. BEULAH enters carrying a sugar bowl chocked full of sweeteners.)

BEULAH. Here you are. *(She places the sugar bowl on the coffee table.)*

CECIL. Thank you, ma'am.

BEULAH *(correcting him)*. Uh-uh. *(She wags a finger.)* Mom.

CECIL. Thank you…Mom.

(PUG sweetens his tea.)

BEULAH. Music to my ears. And I know the girls are going to be SO excited.

CECIL. Oh, I'm sure once you tell them… Girls?

BEULAH. Your sisters! You have sisters, three of them. *(She looks at her wristwatch.)*

PUG. Hear that, Cecil…I mean Jimmy. You have a whole family.

CECIL. Yeah, yeah. *(To BEULAH.)* I have sisters?

BEULAH. I called them right after Officer Doughberg left. They should be here any minute.

(At that moment, JOAN enters through the front door.)

BEULAH. Joan!

CECIL *(eyes widen)*. Wow, she is gorgeous! *(Now playing the part of the brother he jumps to his feet.)* Joan! *(He crosses to her with outstretched arms.)* Joan, dear Joan, my sweet sister Joan. It's me! Jimmy! *(He hugs her. BEULAH smiles and shakes her head.)* Your own Jimmy.

JOAN. Will you let go of me! *(She shoves CECIL away.)*

CECIL. What? Is this any way to treat your long-lost brother-dear?

JOAN. I'm NOT your sister!

CECIL. Hah?

BEULAH *(moves to CECIL)*. No, no, this is my technician. Joan Crandall.

CECIL. Oh, I beg your pardon. My mistake. *(Curiously.)* Technician?

JOAN *(eying CECIL suspiciously)*. Mortician and embalmer.

CECIL. You're awfully pretty for that job.

JOAN *(heard this one before)*. Uh huh.

CECIL. I would've figured you for a model or movie star.

JOAN *(sarcastically)*. Oh, I gave all that up because I like to be around graveyards. *(She sees PUG.)* And who's he?

PUG *(rises)*. 'Evening!

BEULAH. He's a friend of Jimmy's. Why are you here?

(PUG sits again and continues to snack.)

JOAN. I got a call from Alfred. *(She circles CECIL looking over him from head to foot.)*

BEULAH. Officer Doughberg called you?

JOAN. He told me what went on here tonight. *(She looks at BEULAH.)* Tonight of all nights.

CECIL. Why tonight, what's happening tonight?

BEULAH. Just don't worry your head about it, Jimmy. Now that you're here that should straighten things out.

CECIL. Straighten WHAT things out? *(He looks back at JOAN.)* What ARE you looking for?!

JOAN *(moves to BEULAH)*. Mrs. Beulah, if I didn't know you better I'd swear you cooked up this whole thing.

CECIL. What thing?

BEULAH. How do you mean?

JOAN. Some trick to stall everything.

BEULAH. Now you KNOW I would never do any such thing.

CECIL. What thing?

BEULAH. I trust my girls implicitly and I know they're just thinking of what's best all around.

JOAN. Right. And what're they going to say when they meet him?

PUG. What thing?

BEULAH *(to PUG)*. They want me to sell the business.

CECIL *(to himself)*. Now what was I saying wrong?

JOAN. Whatever. *(She turns to CECIL.)* You want to explain who you really are?

BEULAH *(appalled)*. Joan!

JOAN. Why you showed up here tonight? How you got in here? And what you're REALLY up to?

CECIL. Hey! If you'll just give me a chance to get in a word edgewise!

JOAN. Well?

CECIL. Listen, this is new to me, too, but when this lady here—

BEULAH *(correcting him)*. Mom.

CECIL. —when Mom here told me everything it all made sense.

JOAN. Oh, it did?

CECIL. Sure. I mean look at that face. *(He indicates BEULAH.)* Have you ever seen a more honest face?

JOAN. Mrs. Beulah! You CAN'T be serious.

BEULAH. Joan, I ought to know my own son.

CECIL *(to JOAN)*. Sheesh! Can't you cut a guy a little slack? *(He moves to PUG.)*

JOAN. Hey, you think I'M bad wait till you meet the others. Your…sisters?

BEULAH. Now what makes you say such a thing? I just KNOW they'll be as jubilant as I am.

JOAN. Are we talking about the same people?

(At that moment, ZELDA enters through the front door.)

BEULAH. Zelda, you won't believe it, you just won't believe it.

JOAN. THERE'S an understatement.

ZELDA. Oh, where IS he, where is my dear Jimmy?

(CECIL cautiously raises a hand.)

BEULAH. Right over there.

(ZELDA tentatively crosses to CECIL.)

ZELDA. Jimmy?

CECIL *(cautiously)*. Yes?

ZELDA. It's so good to have you home again. *(Meekly she holds out her arms and clumsily hugs him.)*

JOAN *(surprised)*. Huh?

CECIL *(smiles, at JOAN)*. Hey, this ain't so tough.

BEULAH. Give him a real hug, Zelda.

ZELDA. Oh, sorry. *(She hugs CECIL again, again it is a clumsy attempt.)*

CECIL. I'm not going to break you know.

ZELDA *(breaks the hug)*. Oh, sorry. *(She sees PUG.)* Who's he? If I may ask.

PUG *(rises)*. S'up?

CECIL. He's a friend of mine. *(He motions PUG to sit down, which he does.)* And you are sister Zelda.

ZELDA *(to BEULAH)*. Oh, Mother, you must be so happy.
BEULAH. You just cannot imagine.
JOAN *(moves to ZELDA)*. Zelda, you BELIEVE HIM?
ZELDA. Yes. *(A beat.)* Sorry.
BEULAH. Where are the others?
ZELDA. Right behind me.

(At that moment, IMOGENE enters through the front door. She is pale and dressed completely in black.)

IMOGENE. What a lovely night out. Cold, drizzling rain. The fog is positively delicious.
PUG *(sees IMOGENE)*. What in the name of Boris Karloff is that?

(CECIL motions PUG to keep quiet.)

BEULAH. Imogene. Here's your baby brother. *(She indicates CECIL.)*
IMOGENE *(moves slowly to CECIL)*. James, dear James, returned home. "Home is the hunter home from the hill and sailor home from the sea."
CECIL. I have missed you SO much, sister Imogene! *(He holds out his arms.)*
ZELDA. Isn't it wonderful, Imogene? *(IMOGENE shoots her a dirty look.)* I mean, if YOU think it is.
IMOGENE. Diabolical I'd say. *(She reaches over and shakes CECIL's hand.)* Lovely to have you back home, James.
BEULAH *(to CECIL)*. She'd give you a hug but she doesn't like to touch people.

IMOGENE. Not while they're alive, in any case. *(She sees PUG.)* Who's he?

PUG *(rises)*. We'll get to him in a minute. *(He sits and keeps snacking, all the while watching the others.)*

JOAN. I don't BELIEVE this!

BEULAH *(moves to JOAN)*. What's not to believe?

JOAN *(indicates the sisters)*. Them! *(An aside to BEULAH.)* They're up to something.

(At that moment, GRETCHEN enters through the front door. She is smartly dressed.)

GRETCHEN. Okay, what's the story here? *(She points to PUG.)* Is that him?

PUG *(half rises)*. Don't get up. *(He sits again.)*

BEULAH. No, that's him with Imogene.

CECIL *(to IMOGENE)*. And she's—?

IMOGENE. Gretchen, the oldest.

(CECIL rushes over to GRETCHEN with outstretched arms.)

CECIL. Sister Gretchen!

GRETCHEN *(holds a hand up)*. Please! The formalities. *(She eyes him up and down.)* I don't know you and you don't know me. Let's proceed from that basis, shall we?

BEULAH. Now, Gretchen, play nice.

GRETCHEN. Oh, Mother. I'm not so easily swayed by sentiment as SOME people.

BEULAH. I'm telling you he is your baby brother. And there's no sentiment about it.

GRETCHEN. So you say. A moment. *(She puts an arm about CECIL and pulls him downstage. She speaks to him quietly in a more brutal voice.)* Listen, pal, I don't know who you really are but trust me. First chance I get I'm going to gut you like a fish and make it look like an accident.

(CECIL stares at her in disbelief and then turns to BEULAH.)

CECIL *(a whining child)*. MOM!

BEULAH *(moves to them)*. Okay, you two, now there'll be plenty of time for us to catch up.

GRETCHEN. Now, Mother, somebody has to have their feet on the ground around this place. You know, after Father died—

BEULAH. Yes, yes, and you had to take over a lot of his responsibilities. *(She moves to CECIL.)* But now Jimmy's home and he can take over from now on.

GRETCHEN. That's what I thought.

(IMOGENE and ZELDA move to GRETCHEN.)

ZELDA. Isn't it wonderful?

IMOGENE *(to ZELDA)*. Will you shut up?

ZELDA. Sorry.

GRETCHEN *(looks at JOAN)*. Why are you here?

JOAN. I got a call from Alfred and he thought—

GRETCHEN *(pointedly)*. Well, this is a family matter, don't you think?

JOAN. I'm sorry, EXCUSE me!

BEULAH. Gretchen, you stop that this minute! *(She moves to JOAN.)* Joan, she didn't mean anything by that, she was just—

JOAN. No, it's quite all right. *(She glares at GRETCHEN.)* I'm used to her. *(Back to BEULAH.)* I need to get back home anyway. *(She opens the front door.)*

CECIL. Nice to meet you!

JOAN. Whatever. *(She exits.)*

GRETCHEN. Would it be all right if I talked with my sisters a moment? *(For CECIL's benefit.)* In private, *s'il vous plaît?*

BEULAH. You just behave. All of you. *(She moves to CECIL.)* Let's go into my office here and I'll show you all about the business.

CECIL. Sure. *(For the others benefit.)* Mom! *(He looks at PUG.)* Parnell?

PUG *(rises)*. Right behind you…Jimbo.

BEULAH. This is all like a wonderful dream. *(She holds CECIL's face in her hand and exits into the manager's office.)*

(CECIL looks at the others, sniffs indignantly and exits. PUG starts to move but then grabs another sandwich and exits.)

ZELDA. Why did you call us up and ask us to be nice to him? *(GRETCHEN looks at her.)* I mean, if you'd care to tell us, that's all I meant. I wasn't trying to—

GRETCHEN. Oh, stop sniveling, Zelda!

IMOGENE. She does have a point, Gretchen. I went out of my way to welcome him into our little circle.

ZELDA. She really did! I've never seen Imogene so warm and friendly.

IMOGENE. Don't get used to it. *(To GRETCHEN.)* If you have some nefarious plan then pray tell us what it is.

GRETCHEN. It's quite simple. I want that imposter to think you're on HIS side. THAT way maybe he'll make a mistake and we can expose him. I just acted the way Mother would expect out of me. We don't want to upset her at this late stage in the game.

ZELDA. And now what?

IMOGENE. Yes, what's our next move?

GRETCHEN. Easy. We get rid of him. *(She looks out with a sinister look on her face.)* One way or another...we get rid of him.

ZELDA. How? *(The other two sisters glare at her.)* Sorry.

(LIGHTS black out.)

Scene Three

(It is the next morning. JOAN is sitting at the desk working on the computer. Officer DOUGHBERG is on the other side of the desk.)

DOUGHBERG. I tell you that guy is up to no good. I can feel it. *(He points to his stomach.)* Right here.

JOAN *(trying to work)*. Right.

DOUGHBERG. It's called a "gut feeling." Instinct. All good detectives have it. They don't need any proof, any clues, they can FEEL it. *(Again he points to his stom-*

ach.) Right here, right in the old breadbox. Yessir, gut feeling. *(He rubs his stomach.)* Maybe I'm hungry?

JOAN. Alfred, I'm trying to work here. *(She keeps typing.)*

DOUGHBERG *(leans over the desk)*. I'm telling you, Joanie-bunny, I crack one good case, one BIG case and I'm a cinch for a promotion.

JOAN *(stops typing and look up)*. Joanie-bunny?

DOUGHBERG. Yeah, I thought since you and me was going together I needed to give you a pet name.

JOAN. Well, that sounds like one you'd give a pet. *(She continues typing.)*

DOUGHBERG. Don't like it, huh? I'll work on it.

JOAN. You do that.

DOUGHBERG *(eyes widen)*. Say, maybe they'd finally promote me to lieutenant! Then I could go plain clothes. Wouldn't that be great? *(No response from JOAN.)* Huh, wouldn't that be wonderful? Joanie-bear?

JOAN *(stops and again looks at him)*. Will you stop?

DOUGHBERG *(indicates himself)*. You just watch this old cop for the next few days and will YOU be proud of me.

JOAN *(rises)*. Alfred, I already AM proud of you. You don't need to go taking any chances just to impress me, you know.

(Officer DOUGHBERG moves behind the desk, takes JOAN's hand and gently pulls her to him)

DOUGHBERG. Hey, this is for the both of us. I get a promotion it means a boost in salary. Then I can support you in style.

JOAN. Are you proposing?

DOUGHBERG *(taken aback)*. Huh?

JOAN. Well, you said you want to support me in style.

DOUGHBERG. Oh, well, what I meant—

JOAN *(laughing)*. Relax, I was only kidding you. *(She turns away.)*

DOUGHBERG *(pulls her gently back to him)*. Well, what if I was?

JOAN. Was what?

DOUGHBERG. Proposing.

JOAN. That's not a "what if" type of question, is it?

DOUGHBERG. No, I just mean… Say! That's an old suspect trick. Answer a question WITH a question.

JOAN. And just WHAT am I suspected of?

DOUGHBERG. I'll tell you, you're…you did it again!

(JOAN hugs Officer DOUGHBERG just as CECIL enters through the front door. He is now wearing a very nice, well-tailored suit.)

CECIL. Well, well, I DO hope I'm not interrupting anything here.

(JOAN and Officer DOUGHBERG break their clinch. JOAN moves back to the computer.)

DOUGHBERG. You are!

CECIL. I DO beg your pardon, Officer.

DOUGHBERG. Say, you never DID say how you got in here last night?

CECIL. Huh? Oh, THAT! Well, the…the front door wasn't locked. I just walked in.

DOUGHBERG. So you say.

CECIL. You don't believe me, just ask Mrs.—Mom!

JOAN *(looking at CECIL)*. Aren't you dressed to kill?

CECIL *(leans in to JOAN)*. Don't give him any ideas. *(He indicates Officer DOUGHBERG.)*

JOAN. Where'd you get the suit?

CECIL. Mom gave it to me. *(He moves away from the desk.)* Said it belonged to Dad. And it fits me to a T. Don't you think? *(He strikes two or three model poses.)*

JOAN. That doesn't mean anything.

DOUGHBERG. I need to get back to work. *(To CECIL.)* And you! I got my eye on you.

CECIL. Say, that really gives me a very secure feeling, knowing that you're watching out for me. *(He turns away and straightens his cuffs.)*

DOUGHBERG. That's right, keep making with the jokes. *(He leans over and kisses JOAN on the cheek. He then speaks softly to her.)* Listen, if you can get me something with his fingerprints on it I can run them.

JOAN. Fingerprints?

(This catches CECIL's attention and he looks at Officer DOUGHBERG curiously.)

DOUGHBERG. I'll be around. *(He moves to the front door. Then suddenly shoots a look at CECIL, who turns away and whistles idly. He then looks at JOAN.)* See you later, Joanie-dumpling. *(He exits as JOAN shudders.)*

CECIL. Joanie-dumpling?

JOAN. He's hungry, leave him alone. *(She begins typing again.)*

CECIL. You know, I don't think he likes me.

JOAN. Just him? *(She begins typing again.)*

CECIL *(moves to JOAN)*. Oh, you too.

JOAN. No point in going into that. It doesn't make any difference what I think.

CECIL *(leans in to JOAN)*. And what would you say it I said it does…to me.

JOAN. Then I'd say don't worry about it.

CECIL. Well, then I'd say I'm the kind of guy who DOES worry about things like that.

JOAN. Then I'D say that's YOUR problem.

CECIL. Then I'D say what can I do to change your mind?

JOAN *(stops typing)*. I'd say nothing.

CECIL *(straightens up)*. Good thing we didn't have that conversation.

(At that moment, PUG enters through the L door and watches CECIL and JOAN.)

JOAN *(softening a bit)*. Look, I don't mean to sound rude but I have all this work to do. *(She gathers up some papers.)*

CECIL. But you really think I'm up to no good?

JOAN. I didn't say that.

CECIL. You haven't really given me a chance, you know.

(JOAN rises and moves around the desk.)

JOAN. What do you expect? You show up out of the blue, Mrs. Beulah says you're her son and you immediately take advantage of her! *(She pokes CECIL in the chest.)* Listen, whoever you are, I think the world of her and I'd do ANYTHING, and I mean ANYTHING to see she doesn't get hurt.

CECIL. And what would you say if I said the same thing?

JOAN. Then I'D say...oh, don't start THAT again.

CECIL. But I MEAN that. I don't want to hurt the old...I mean Mom!

JOAN *(pointedly)*. Then I'D say that's what I expected you to say! *(She then moves to the double doors.)*

CECIL. I thought you'd say that. *(JOAN shakes her head and exits. CECIL rushes up to the door as it closes.)* If you'd just let me talk to you, just for a minute or two— *(The door is shut. He turns and sees PUG.)* She's nuts about me.

PUG. Yeah, she probably went to get a gun. *(He moves to CECIL.)* I WONDERED why we was sticking.

CECIL. What do you mean by that?

PUG. What do you mean by that, he says, innocent as a nerd on his first date.

CECIL. What? *(He indicates the double doors.)* You mean her?

PUG. I don't mean the Easter Bunny. Are you out of your mind?

CECIL. Pug, I was just playing her. You know, cozying up to her so she'll be on our side.

PUG. That's not what it looked like to me.

CECIL. You just let me worry about that.

PUG. Oh fine. You can worry about that and I can worry about all those other things. Like we'll get found out or we'll get arrested, you know, small potatoes.

CECIL. There IS one other thing that does worry me, however. The same problem we always run into.

PUG. They're smarter than us?

CECIL. No! *(He thinks.)* Well? *(He shakes his head.)* No! Look, as confidence men we HAVE to win their confidence, right?

PUG. Win their confidence? Listen, I wouldn't be surprised if that gang of sisters was planning on croaking the both of us.

CECIL. What?

PUG. I mean, did you get a load of that clutch? One of them looks like somebody forgot to nail down a coffin lid somewhere. And that other one keeps apologizing to everybody for everything? I bet she's got a whole CROWD of skeletons in the closet. Then there's what's-her-name, that hoity-toity one. One of those dames from *Who's Who?* who looked at us like we're from *What's That?*

CECIL. She was a tad cold, wasn't she?

PUG. And what'd she say to you?

CECIL. I try not to think about it. Call it an unveiled threat.

PUG. Cecil, let's blow this burg before it's too late. I'm begging you.

CECIL. Oh, this is all in your imagination. *(He moves to the double doors and looks at them.)*

PUG. My imagination? Those three are planning our demise even as we speak.

CECIL. Oh, get serious. What would those dames know about knocking somebody off? They wouldn't know the first thing about it.

PUG. How you figger?

CECIL. For instance, where would they hide the bodies?

(CECIL stares at PUG. Slowly the two of them look around the room and then stare out as it dawns on them.)

PUG. Well, you know what they say. Location, location, location.

(At that moment, HUNTER enters through the front door. He is smartly dressed, complete with a Homburg, and is carrying a briefcase.)

HUNTER *(mumbling to himself)*. I don't know why I put myself through this, I'm getting too old for this kind of aggravation. I should've retired years ago. People just don't know what I go through. And do they care when I try to tell them? No siree bob. And listen to me—who says "no siree bob" anymore? *(He takes off his hat and plops it on the desk. He then places the briefcase next to the chair facing the desk, all the time never stopping his muttering.)* I'm an anachronism, that's what I am, I ought to face it. I don't belong to this age. It's just one crisis after another and everybody thinks I have the answers? And when I don't they want to sue ME! And who gave them that idea to begin with? ME! *(He plops in the chair, crosses his arms and looks over at CECIL and PUG.)* You lose somebody?

CECIL. Why, you find somebody?

HUNTER. Who are you?

CECIL. I was just about to ask you the same thing.

HUNTER. Uh-uh, witness is being hostile; I asked you first.

CECIL & PUG *(look at each other)*. Lawyer!

PUG *(to CECIL)*. Didn't I tell you we should blow!

CECIL *(to HUNTER)*. Let's just say I'm one of the family.

HUNTER. You have my undying sympathy. *(He rises, places his briefcase on the desk and opens it.)* Is Beulah here; I have those contracts for her to sign. *(He pulls out three contracts.)*

CECIL *(moves to HUNTER)*. No, but she should be here soon. Her daughters may be around.

(Wide-eyed, HUNTER looks around.)

HUNTER *(panicking)*. Where?! Are they here?! You can tell me, I need to prepare myself. Oh, how I wish I drank.

CECIL. Take it easy, sir.

HUNTER. That's the LAST thing I need today is to put up with that unholy trio. How a lovely lady like Beulah Meadows could've hatched that batch of unmerciful harpies is beyond me. Did you EVER meet a more unrepentant gang of conniving crones in your life?

CECIL *(pats HUNTER on the back)*. Is there anything I can do?

HUNTER. Yes, God bless you! *(He shoves the contacts at CECIL.)* Take these and give them to Mrs. Meadows; there's a good fellow. *(He quickly snaps his briefcase shut.)*

CECIL. Is that legal?

HUNTER. Legal schmegal, just do an old man a favor!

CECIL. What ARE they?

HUNTER. They're for the sale of Green Meadows to the Fairview Memorial Funeral chain.

CECIL. Oh, ARE they? *(He eyes the contracts.)*

(At that moment, JOAN enters through the double doors.)

JOAN. I thought I heard you come in, Mr. Derossett. *(She moves to HUNTER.)*

HUNTER. Joan! Good, you're here. *(He quickly snatches the contracts from CECIL and shoves them at JOAN.)* Here's the contracts. Get Mrs. Meadows to sign them and mail them back to me.

JOAN. Don't you want to go over them with the family?

HUNTER. That's the nastiest thing you've ever said to me.

JOAN. I see you've met him. *(She indicates CECIL.)*

CECIL. Sorta. *(He reaches for the contracts.)* Can I have a look at those again?

JOAN *(pulling away)*. He gave them to me. *(To HUNTER.)* I guess he told you who he was?

HUNTER. I don't care.

JOAN. Oh? *(She looks at CECIL.)* Didn't you tell him what you told us, that you're Jimmy?

CECIL. I didn't have a chance.

HUNTER. Jimmy?!

JOAN. Yes. He CLAIMS to be Mrs. Beulah's missing son.

(On hearing this, HUNTER looks at CECIL and then breaks out into gales of laughter.)

PUG. Well, he took it better than I thought he would. *(He moves to the others.)*

JOAN. Mr. Derossett, will you get hold of yourself?

HUNTER *(trying to control himself)*. Sorry. *(Still laughing he again sits in the chair.)* This is wonderful! This is manna from Heaven!

JOAN *(amazed).* Then you believe him?

HUNTER. Hey, innocent until proven guilty, that's written somewhere. *(He thinks.)* I used to know that stuff.

JOAN. But all we have is Mrs. Beulah's identification and his word. *(She eyes CECIL.)* For what that's worth.

HUNTER. Who cares?! *(He smiles broadly.)* I bet this really stuck in Gretchen's craw! *(He looks at CECIL.)* Does she know? Tell me she doesn't, PLEASE! I just HAVE to see her face when she hears the news.

JOAN. She knows.

HUNTER. RATS! Big, stinking, hairy rats. DOUBLE RATS! I would've paid dearly to have seen that. And I'm talking serious cash here.

(At that moment, BEULAH enters through the front door.)

JOAN. Good morning, Mrs. Beulah.

BEULAH. And good morning, Joan. Isn't it a lovely day? Oh, Hunter!

HUNTER. Beulah! *(He crosses to her.)* How lovely you look?

BEULAH. Oh, you always were a silver-tongued sort. I see you've met Jimmy.

CECIL. Yes, and he took it rather well, I thought.

PUG. It was like somebody tickled a hyena with a feather.

BEULAH *(straightens CECIL's collar and admires him).* Doesn't he look nice in his father's suit? I LOVE a well-dressed man.

(HUNTER grabs the contracts from JOAN and hands them to BEULAH.)

HUNTER. Here are those contracts for you to sign.

BEULAH. What contracts?

HUNTER. For the sale of Green Meadows to the Fairview Memorial—

BEULAH. Oh, that's all off now.

JOAN. What?

BEULAH. Since Jimmy has returned home I just KNOW he'll get us back on our feet in no time.

CECIL. Uh, ma'am, I don't—

BEULAH *(correcting him)*. Mom!

JOAN. Have you told your daughters yet? About you not wanting to sell now?

BEULAH. Well, no. *(She moves to HUNTER.)* I thought you'd be kind enough to fill them in on that?

HUNTER *(after a long pause)*. HAH!

BEULAH. After all, I KNOW they'll have LOTS of questions and you know all the facts in the case. *(She moves to the manager's door.)* Now I need to take care of a few things before my hair appointment.

JOAN *(indicating CECIL)*. Mrs. Beulah, don't you think you ought to make SURE of who he is before—

BEULAH *(stops at the door)*. My mind is made up. Hunter, the girls will be here at two. You can talk to them then. *(She exits.)*

(HUNTER turns away. He now has a very mournful look on his face.)

JOAN *(to CECIL)*. Well, I hope you're happy! *(She moves to the manager's door.)* Mrs. Beulah, if you'll just listen to me a minute— *(She exits out the door.)*

PUG *(to CECIL)*. NOW what do we do?

CECIL. I'm thinking, I'm thinking!

HUNTER. I have to come BACK?! I have to tell them, those three vicious, vindictive vipers?! *(He falls in the chair again and begins sobbing quietly.)*

CECIL. We need to hear what goes on at that meeting.

PUG. How? They're not going to say anything with you and me there.

CECIL. Maybe we don't HAVE to be there.

PUG. Oh, well as long as you know what we're doing.

(PUG turns and sees HUNTER. He then pulls out a handkerchief and moves to HUNTER. He holds out the handkerchief which HUNTER takes and blows his nose loudly. LIGHTS black out.)

Scene Four

(It is just before two o'clock that afternoon. IMOGENE and ZELDA are sitting on the sofa while GRETCHEN is sitting in the chair next to the sofa. HUNTER is facing them, his briefcase on the coffee table, holding the contracts and wincing. The ladies stare at him in horror for a medium pause.)

GRETCHEN & IMOGENE *(viciously)*. WHAT?!

ZELDA *(looks away)*. Oh dear.

HUNTER. You all heard me, the deal is off. *(He tugs at his collar nervously.)*

GRETCHEN *(jumps to her feet)*. But it's all set!

HUNTER. Then it will just have to be upset.

GRETCHEN. And just WHEN did THIS happen?

HUNTER. This morning. Your mother—

GRETCHEN. I KNEW it! That...that CHARLATAN shows up and Mother goes off the deep end.

ZELDA. Oh dear.

HUNTER. Your mother—

GRETCHEN. I KNEW he was up to something!

IMOGENE *(to ZELDA)*. I had a bad feeling; it started this morning. When I went to my car a crow was perched on the hood. You know what that's a sign of?

ZELDA. He needed a ride to town?

IMOGENE. It's an omen and a black one at that.

GRETCHEN. Imogene, will you leave off all that hocus-pocus for two minutes and listen to me!

HUNTER. Your mother—

GRETCHEN. It's blackmail, that's what he's up to. He's going to blackmail us, you just wait and see.

IMOGENE *(rising slowly)*. Hocus-pocus? Is THAT what you call it? *(She points a finger at GRETCHEN.)* I'll have you know that I have guided my life by the natural signs and omens given to those of us who know how to read them!

GRETCHEN. And just LOOK where it's got you! YOU need the money as bad as I do.

IMOGENE. Oh? Running a little short, are we? I suppose trying to keep up that phony upper-class façade of yours CAN be expensive. What's the matter; your country club fee is due again and you're strapped?

HUNTER. Your mother—

ZELDA. Maybe it's for the best.

(GRETCHEN and IMOGENE turn on her. She sinks into the sofa.)

GRETCHEN. Listen, Cordelia! DON'T think you're going to win points by playing on her sympathies! And will you SIT UP! *(ZELDA stiffens her posture, immediately.)*

IMOGENE *(to ZELDA)*. You should take yourself in hand. What did your horoscope say today?

HUNTER *(defiantly)*. YOUR MOTHER— *(He stops. The others turn and look at him.)* Oh, I get to talk now?

GRETCHEN. What could you possibly say that's any help?

HUNTER. Your mother is the only one who, by rights, can sell this establishment, and if she chooses not to that's her affair.

GRETCHEN. But she's not thinking clearly, can't you see that?

IMOGENE. Maybe we should read HER horoscope?

ZELDA. You think that would help?

IMOGENE. After all, if her guiding planets are not lined up with the waxing and waning of the moon it just may be we're here on the wrong day.

GRETCHEN. Will you SHUT UP?! *(ZELDA starts to speak.)* You, too. You two just keep your mouths shut until I figure this out. And don't you say ANYTHING to Mother until I say so! As always, I have to be the level-headed one of the family.

IMOGENE. But—

GRETCHEN. I said SHUT UP!

HUNTER. Hey, take it EASY, can't you?! *(GRETCHEN looks at him.)* Just because Hitler's dead doesn't mean the job's open!

GRETCHEN. Oh, and I suppose YOU believe that con artist is really Jimmy?

HUNTER. Not my place to say. I can only acquiesce to my client's wishes. And, IN THIS CASE, my client is Beulah Meadows. *(He looks up.)* May God help her.

IMOGENE *(to GRETCHEN)*. Well, what are we going to do?

GRETCHEN. You mean, what am I going to do? I always have to do the thinking for you two. I just wonder where you'd be without me.

HUNTER *(to himself)*. In a bar somewhere gleefully toasting their good luck.

GRETCHEN *(turns to HUNTER)*. What was that?

HUNTER. I said it seems to me that you three are out of luck.

ZELDA. But what if he really IS Jimmy?

GRETCHEN. And what if donkeys can fly. *(Pointedly, to IMOGENE.)* What sort of omen would THAT be? *(IMOGENE starts to answer but is interrupted by GRETCHEN.)* There's GOT to be a way to rectify all this.

(At that moment, JOAN enters through the double doors and crosses to the desk. The others watch her in silence. She picks up a folder and turns to see the others. She forces a smile.)

JOAN. I'm fine, thank you. *(She then exits out the double doors, all the while under the watchful eyes of the sisters.)*

HUNTER. Anyway, I've now exhausted my duties here and leave the lot of you with yourselves. *(He opens his briefcase and deposits the contacts.)* And I can't think of anyone more deserving of such a curse. *(He slams his case.)*

GRETCHEN. Curses are more in Imogene's department.

IMOGENE. And just what's THAT supposed to mean?

ZELDA. Please, let's not fight with each other; it gives me a migraine.

GRETCHEN. Oh, will you STOP!

ZELDA. I would, but how?

GRETCHEN. It's all in your mind, can't you see that?

(HUNTER picks up his briefcase and moves to the front door.)

HUNTER *(to himself)*. What a way to make a living! I should've been a plumber. Or an exterminator. At least, those guys get to empty the house before they can go to work. They don't have to listen to a bunch of greedy, grasping gargoyles.

GRETCHEN *(an inspiration)*. All in your mind! Wait a minute. Mother really ISN'T thinking clearly, is she?

(HUNTER is just about to grab the doorknob and stops in his tracks.)

IMOGENE. What do you mean?

GRETCHEN. I MEAN she thinks that guy is Jimmy, right? So...she's simply not in her right mind.

HUNTER. Hah? *(He turns and looks at the ladies.)*

ZELDA. Just because she thinks that?

IMOGENE *(catching on)*. Oh! I get it. *(She moves to GRETCHEN.)* If that were to come out, about her having delusions, then maybe—

GRETCHEN. Maybe she'd have to be taken care of. And someone ELSE would be given power of attorney.

HUNTER. Wait, wait, wait. *(He moves to the ladies.)*

IMOGENE *(to GRETCHEN)*. And that would be you, right?

GRETCHEN. Think of it. I take over and the whole deal can be saved; we can STILL sell this old barn.

IMOGENE. Yes. And not only the funeral home but also her house!

GRETCHEN. Way ahead of you. After all, she'd have to be put some place where she can be taken care of. After all, running this business obviously has taken its toll.

HUNTER. You can't DO that!

GRETCHEN. Why not? We're her daughters, so who else would be in a better position.

ZELDA *(moves to the others)*. Mother is not crazy!

GRETCHEN. What would you call someone who picks up a bum off the street and thinks he's her son!

HUNTER. It's not that easy. There's...there's legalities. Also, you'd need a psychiatrist's report on her.

GRETCHEN. So? What's the problem? We get a reliable analyst and all Mother has to do is talk to her. The minute she opens her mouth about Jimmy—

IMOGENE. You know one? A psychiatrist?

GRETCHEN. Not personally, but there's one I've heard about at the club. Uh...Phoebe Wallenstein. That's her. I'll put in a call to her right away.

IMOGENE. And once we get her report the only thing left to do is get everything down on paper, drawn up legally.

GRETCHEN. Right. *(The ladies all turn to HUNTER.)*

HUNTER. What? ME?! Oh no! I won't have any part of this. *(He rushes to the front door.)*

GRETCHEN. You HAVE to! *(The three ladies all follow him.)* We have you on retainer!

HUNTER. Not for this! Find yourself another sucker! *(He exits out the door.)*

IMOGENE. Wouldn't that mean you're breaking your contract with the family!

GRETCHEN. How'd THAT sound in court!

(GRETCHEN and IMOGENE exit after him.)

ZELDA. But this just isn't right! *(She exits after them.)*

(After a slight pause, CECIL looks through the L door. He has his cell phone to his ear. He looks behind him.)

CECIL. They're gone. *(He enters, followed by PUG.)*

PUG. Well, now we know what they're up to.

CECIL. I heard. Get your cell phone.

(PUG moves to the sofa and, bending down, he retrieves his cell phone from under it.)

PUG. Fat lot we can do about it.

CECIL *(pockets his cell phone)*. Keep your shirt on, I'm thinking.

PUG. He's thinking. It's your thinking that got us IN this mess. *(He pockets his cell phone.)*

CECIL. I wouldn't call it a mess.

PUG. Oh, really? Let's recap your plan. You pretend to be this Jimmy and, according to your plan, they'd never prove you're not Jimmy. NOW, they're going to put that old lady away unless you CAN prove you ARE Jimmy.

You can look that up in the dictionary…under the word MESS!

(Unseen by the two men JOAN opens the double doors and is about to enter. When she sees them she is just about to leave.)

CECIL. I'm thinking, I said; give me a chance here.
PUG. What's to think about, let's BLOW!

(On hearing this, JOAN stops and listens to them.)

CECIL. NO!
PUG. What?
CECIL. We are NOT running out, not now, anyway.
PUG. Can you think of a better time to skedaddle?
CECIL. I am NOT going to leave that wonderful old woman to those three vicious vampires.

(On hearing this, JOAN's eyes widen and she looks at CECIL with more sympathy.)

PUG. Now you're starting to sound like that lawyer guy.
CECIL. Look, you want to take a hike, go ahead, but I'm sticking.
PUG *(relenting)*. No. *(Sarcastically.)* We need to stay together for the children.
CECIL. Can you believe her own daughters want to have her committed?!
JOAN. WHAT?

(CECIL and PUG turn and see JOAN.)

CECIL. Joan!

JOAN *(moves to them)*. They're going to try to have Mrs. Beulah committed?!

PUG. How much did you hear?

JOAN. Just that. *(CECIL and PUG look at each other and let out a sigh of relief.)* I didn't think they'd stoop THAT low. *(She starts to leave then stops. She turns back to CECIL.)* You know maybe I was wrong about you. *(She moves to the double doors then turns back.)* Maybe. *(She exits.)*

CECIL *(smiling)*. You hear that?

PUG. I heard, I heard! So? What's our next move?

CECIL *(thinks a minute then snaps his fingers)*. What we need here...is a diversion. *(He resumes his thoughts.)*

PUG. What KIND of diversion? *(He gets no response from CECIL.)* Huh? What are you thinking? *(Again no response. He snaps his fingers in front of CECIL's face.)* Cecil? Cecil! Are you listening to me? CECIL!

(LIGHTS black out.)

END OF ACT ONE

ACT TWO

Scene One

(It is the next day. HUNTER and BEULAH sit on the sofa while JOAN works at the desk, looking every so often at the couple.)

HUNTER. So now you know the whole story. Those... daughters of yours are plotting against you and if they have their way—

BEULAH. Don't say "plotting against me." They're just looking at all avenues now that things have changed. And I just cannot believe they're planning on putting me in some home.

HUNTER. I heard them myself! Things have changed, all right, and Gretchen sees it as this new guy usurping her power.

BEULAH. His name is Jimmy. And you know that Gretchen has always been the careful one. Especially after her father died. I'll have a word or two with her. I'm sure she'll see things my way.

HUNTER. WHEN has she EVER seen things your way?

BEULAH. Well... *(She is stuck for an answer.)* Oh, you have me all flustered now and I simply cannot think.

HUNTER. Look, it all hinges on Jimmy. Since he showed up this whole thing has come to a head. The sale of the business now hangs in the balance and those...your daughters don't like it. You can hear it in Gretchen's voice. When she speaks about it you can hear the cash registers clicking over.

BEULAH. What are you trying to say?

HUNTER. Simply this. When you're asked—

BEULAH. Asked by whom?

HUNTER. ANYbody! When you're asked about Jimmy simply say he REMINDS you of your son. Or he LOOKS LIKE your son. That way—

(BEULAH rises and takes on a stern expression.)

BEULAH *(indignantly)*. You mean deny him? Is that what you're saying?

HUNTER. No! No, no, no! *(He looks at her.)* Yes.

BEULAH. You want me to deny my own son?!

HUNTER. Just whenever anyone asks. It'll only be for a short time and—

BEULAH. I'd rather cut off my right arm! *(She moves to the manager's office.)*

HUNTER. Beulah! *(He jumps to his feet.)*

BEULAH *(looks at him)*. I think that is the cruelest thing you've ever said to me! *(She exits.)*

HUNTER *(looks at the door and then, sheepishly, he looks at JOAN)*. I think I just made things worse.

JOAN *(nods)*. Uh huh.

HUNTER *(moves to JOAN)*. If I could just get her to see it my way here, just for a few days, that should be all it takes.

JOAN *(icily)*. Oh? So you're going to HELP her now?

HUNTER. Of course, I— *(He catches her tone.)* What's THAT mean? *(JOAN doesn't answer.)* Okay, why're YOU mad at me?

JOAN. Why're you doing this?

HUNTER. Doing what? You just HEARD me talking to Beulah.

JOAN. I mean, why're you helping Gretchen? She needs an attorney and who does she get? Who goes along with her? You get the same answer to both questions—YOU!

HUNTER. Exactly. At least, I can be here to help Beulah. Maybe I can throw those degenerate sirens a few legal curves, tie them up in red tape. I mean, if I don't do it they'll just get some other attorney to do it. And you know it wouldn't take long for them to find one. *(He leans on the desk.)* I hate lawyers! *(JOAN looks at him quizzically. She is about to speak only to be interrupted by him.)* And, yes, I'm aware of the irony.

(At that moment, CECIL enters through the front door.)

CECIL. Good morning, everyone. And how are we all doing this fine morning? *(He detects the mood of the room.)* Ooh, is it cold in here or is it just you two? *(He pretends to be cold, flapping his arms around his chest.)*

HUNTER. I suppose you've heard the latest?

CECIL. You mean about my sisters planning on ambushing Mom?

HUNTER. Good word for it.

JOAN. You don't seem too upset about it?

HUNTER. Oh, let's just say I have a good feeling about how things will turn out.

JOAN *(rises)*. You DO? *(She moves to CECIL.)* And just what do you have up your sleeve? *(She points to his arm.)*

CECIL. Only an outstretched hand which is very lonely at the moment. *(He takes her hand and cups it with his other hand.)*

JOAN *(gently)*. Oh, your hands are so warm— *(She catches herself.)* Oh, STOP THAT! *(She yanks her hand away. She looks at HUNTER.)* And you. How come you stay around the family?

CECIL *(to HUNTER)*. She said, hoping to change the subject.

HUNTER. I got that.

JOAN. Well? Why DO you stay?

CECIL. I bet I know.

HUNTER. What? What're you talking about?

CECIL *(fingering HUNTER's lapel)*. "One thing I always love is a well-dressed man."

HUNTER. Huh?

CECIL. Something I heard Mom say.

JOAN. Hunter! You've got the hots for Mrs. Beulah!

HUNTER. Oh, don't be ridiculous! I mean, at OUR age? That's…that's…

JOAN. That's the only thing that makes sense.

CECIL. And speaking of sisters, mine is coming over today. *(He casually turns away, waiting for the response to this bombshell.)*

HUNTER. What?

JOAN. What sister?

CECIL. Well, obviously not blood kin, just the lady who raised me.

HUNTER. She's coming HERE?

CECIL. And she should be able to answer any and all questions. *(He moves to JOAN.)* Then, after all that's said and done how about you and I having a little lunch to celebrate?

JOAN. You're THAT confident of how things will turn out?

CECIL. I'll bet you a lunch on it. *(He leans in to her.)* Is it a bet? *(He holds out a hand.)*

JOAN *(shakes his hand)*. Okay, it's a bet. *(They shake hands.)*

CECIL *(to HUNTER)*. You heard her. *(HUNTER nods. CECIL looks at JOAN.)* And anything said in the presence of a lawyer is legally binding.

JOAN. I never heard that.

HUNTER. Me, either. *(He looks at CECIL.)* I like it, though.

(At that moment, PUG enters through the L door.)

PUG *(loudly)*. PSSSSSST!

CECIL. Please excuse me, won't you? My partner is making cartoon noises to get my attention.

(CECIL moves to PUG. JOAN and HUNTER chat quietly among themselves.)

PUG *(quietly, to CECIL)*. It's all set.

CECIL. You made the call then?

PUG *(nods)*. She'll be taking an awful chance, though.

CECIL. She knows the game better'n you or me put together.

(At that moment, GRETCHEN enters through the front door along with IMOGENE and followed by ZELDA.)

GRETCHEN. We'll put an end to this thing today, you just wait and see.

(On seeing them, JOAN sits behind the desk.

IMOGENE. Oh, Hunter! Good, you're here.

GRETCHEN. We need to go over some legalities; I'm sure you understand.

HUNTER. You mean an official and legitimate avenue for you three to rob your mother? I hope you don't mind my use of the word "rob"?

GRETCHEN. Keep a civil tongue in your head. All we want here is your legal advice.

ZELDA. Still, it's always nice to see you, sir. *(HUNTER nods in her direction.)*

IMOGENE *(to ZELDA)*. Oh, just keep quiet and go sit over there. *(She points to the sofa.)*

ZELDA *(meekly)*. Okay. *(She moves to the sofa. To CECIL and PUG.)* Good morning.

CECIL. And a gracious good morning to you, sister Zelda.

ZELDA *(appreciating this)*. Thank you. *(She sits.)*

PUG *(to ZELDA)*. Why do you let them talk to you like that?

ZELDA. Well, they're older and know better.

PUG. Older I can buy, but know better? Shoot, they don't know Jack!

ZELDA. Jack who?

GRETCHEN *(moves to CECIL)*. Now, when is this other sister of yours getting here? The one who's supposed to answer everything?

CECIL. She should be here shortly.

GRETCHEN. Well, until she does we need to speak with our attorney in private. IF you don't mind?!

CECIL *(to PUG)*. I believe they want us to leave.

PUG. The pleasure is all mine.

(CECIL and PUG move to the L door. PUG exits.)

CECIL *(to GRETCHEN)*. You WILL let me know the minute Angelina arrives?

GRETCHEN. Count on it.

CECIL. I'll just see to the refreshments. *(He exits out the door.)*

GRETCHEN *(to HUNTER)*. Now, can we get down to business? *(She and IMOGENE move to the sofa.)*

JOAN *(quietly to HUNTER)*. I don't know what you have planned but good luck.

HUNTER. Watch my dust. *(He moves to the sisters.)*

GRETCHEN. Now, sir, in your best legal opinion what's our first move?

HUNTER. First, it is imperative that you all understand completely what I am about to impart to you.

IMOGENE. That should be no problem.

HUNTER. Good. Now before I can proceed I need to extricate from you as the parties of the first part whether you wish to enter into this agreement under the aegis of *dementia praecox* or *non compos mentis*?

(The sisters look at him and together their mouths drop open.)

IMOGENE. Dowhat?

HUNTER. That must be understood from the outset.

GRETCHEN. Uh…of course. *(She sniffs indignantly.)* I believe we'll go with…that second one.

IMOGENE. You know what that is?

GRETCHEN. Of course. And I personally feel that that first one, that demented…uh…

HUNTER. *Dementia praecox.*

GRETCHEN. Exactly. *(She smiles broadly.)* That one might be harder to prove. Am I right? It's just too… too…

HUNTER. Too Draconian a Brocard?

GRETCHEN. Yes.

(IMOGENE and ZELDA look over at GRETCHEN. On hearing this JOAN smiles, catching on to HUNTER's plan.)

HUNTER. Excellent. Now, to pursue a plea of *non compos mentis* we must first evaluate whether we seek to— *(ZELDA raises her hand.)* Zelda?

ZELDA. What IS *non compos mentis*, anyway?

GRETCHEN. Oh, for heaven's sake, Zelda, don't you know anything?

IMOGENE. Yeah. *(To GRETCHEN.)* You explain it to her.

GRETCHEN. Huh? Oh, well of course. *Non compos…* well, *non* that means no. As in non-fat.

IMOGENE. Why did you look at me when you said that?

GRETCHEN. And *compos*...that's...well, it's...I've heard is used to mean ground as in grounds for a case.

HUNTER. Grounds?

GRETCHEN. Well, compost is when they dig a hole and put in old leaves and table scraps and after awhile—

HUNTER. That's comPOST! *(For the others.)* Simply put, we are trying to establish the basis for your instrument as to whether it's sickness, lunacy or idiocy.

GRETCHEN. I was getting to that.

HUNTER. And once we lay our foundation, then we must decide if we deign to pursue a judgment *non abstante verdicto*. Now there are several pitfalls, if you opt for this constraint, as the judge may introduce *lex ferende*. After all, he is a bastion of *corpus juris*. Also, be cognizant that this instrument, once initiated and granted, is valid up to *articulo mortis*. Now I realize that you may not agree with your counselor, but if that were to take precedence, then I would have no alternative but to appear as an *amicus curiae*. And that, if I may iterate, is the foundation of our contention.

(The ladies all stare at him in total confusion. After a long pause, GRETCHEN turns to her sisters.)

GRETCHEN. Did you all get that?

ZELDA. I'm getting a headache again.

(At that moment, BEULAH enters through the front door.)

BEULAH. Am I too late? Has Jimmy's sister arrived yet?

JOAN. Not yet, Mrs. Beulah.

GRETCHEN *(quietly, to her sisters)*. Not a word to mother about this.

IMOGENE. No problem. *(She indicates HUNTER.)* I didn't understand a word he said.

BEULAH *(moves to the ladies)*. Good, you all are here. Aren't you excited?

HUNTER. I believe you can say they are nonplussed.

IMOGENE. There's that "non" word again.

(HUNTER moves over to JOAN.)

BEULAH. Where's Jimmy?

ZELDA. I think he said something about getting refreshments.

JOAN *(quietly, to HUNTER)*. Nice legal advice.

HUNTER. What legal advice; that was part of a comedy routine I did at a bachelor party last year.

(Just then, PUG enters through the L door. CECIL follows, carrying a tray on which rests a pitcher of iced tea and several glasses.)

CECIL. And here we are. Something to wet our whistles. *(He places the tray on the coffee table.)*

PUG. I thought I heard a car drive up.

CECIL. That must be Angelina. *(He moves to the front door.)*

GRETCHEN *(quietly, to her sisters)*. Okay, just follow my lead. I don't know what this woman is going to say but I'll expose her in short order. Mother may buy that guy's lies, but I'm going to tear this lady apart.

CECIL *(opens the door)*. It IS her. Come in! They're all just dying to meet you.

(ANGELINA enters through the front door. She is dressed head to foot as a nun.)

ANGELINA. And I am all atwitter to meet them as well!

(Everyone else stares at Sister ANGELINA in awe. HUNTER breaks out laughing.)

HUNTER *(composing himself)*. This just gets better and better! *(He breaks into gales of laughter again.)*

(LIGHTS black out.)

Scene Two

(It is an hour later. ANGELINA and BEULAH are now sitting on the couch and drinking tea. GRETCHEN, IMOGENE and ZELDA are now nearby and staring at ANGELINA. CECIL is standing behind the sofa with PUG. JOAN is again sitting at the desk while HUNTER sits in the chair in front of the desk.)

ANGELINA. ...so the next thing I knew there was this woman at our door. Of course, you understand I'm not at liberty to disclose her name, but she brought us Cecil. *(She looks with love at CECIL.)*
BEULAH. Cecil? *(She, too, looks at CECIL.)*

CECIL. That's what she named me; the lady who brought me to Sister Angelina.

ANGELINA. Yes. She told me that he had no memory and simply turned up one day at her door. She knew she couldn't take him home and, well, was afraid to turn him over to the authorities.

BEULAH. Why was that?

ANGELINA. Well, it seems she had a rather checkered past and she felt if she went to the police they'd think she was involved in some sort of kidnapping activities which had gone awry. *(She leans in to BEULAH.)* These are her words, you understand.

BEULAH. Perfectly.

ANGELINA. She had no children of her own and told us that she thought she could look after the boy until he got his memory back. After awhile though she found herself becoming very attached to him and…well…

BEULAH. She brought him to you. *(ANGELINA nods.)*

(CECIL notices PUG wiping his eyes with a handkerchief.)

CECIL. Are you crying?

PUG. That part always gets to me.

GRETCHEN *(grumbling)*. Getting to me, too.

ANGELINA. So when Cecil called me and told me about your fortuitous reunion I was overwhelmed with joy. Well, I've been going on and on now for quite awhile. You must have many questions you'd like to ask me?

BEULAH. Just having him back with us is enough. *(She takes ANGELINA's hand.)* And thank you SO much for taking care of my boy.

(The desk telephone rings and JOAN picks it up.)

ANGELINA. It was no trouble. You see... *(She again looks at CECIL)* ...I've become quite attached to him myself.

JOAN *(into the phone)*. Hello. Oh, yes, she is. Just a moment. *(She looks up.)* Gretchen?

GRETCHEN. What? *(JOAN holds out the receiver. GRETCHEN moves to the desk.)* Now what? *(She takes the receiver and speaks into it.)* Hello? *(She speaks quietly into the phone. JOAN leans in trying to hear but GRETCHEN, seeing this, turns away from her.)*

HUNTER *(rises)*. Well, I guess that answers everything. *(He moves to the sofa.)* So if I'm no longer needed...

BEULAH. Wait, I may have you do one more thing.

HUNTER. For you, anything, m'dear.

ANGELINA. What a gentleman. *(To BEULAH.)* Is he one of the family?

BEULAH. No, he's a lawyer.

ANGELINA *(dismayed)*. Oh, you have my sympathies.

(GRETCHEN motions to IMOGENE and ZELDA to move to her.)

IMOGENE. What?

GRETCHEN. Get over here!

(HUNTER catches this.)

CECIL. Thank you, Sister Angelina, for dropping everything and coming over here on such short notice.

ANGELINA. It was my pleasure.

GRETCHEN *(into the receiver)*. Fine! That will work out perfectly. Goodbye. *(She hands the receiver to JOAN who hangs it up.)*

HUNTER *(to BEULAH)*. They're up to something.

BEULAH. Oh, Hunter, you always think the worst of people.

ANGELINA. I'm sure he cannot help it, being a lawyer.

HUNTER. I was just about to say that. *(He leans in to Sister ANGELINA.)* Getting some inside information from the up above?

ANGELINA. Always.

(Sister ANGELINA and BEULAH rise.)

ANGELINA. So, if there's nothing else I can do for you—?

CECIL. Uh... Say! Sister Angelina, how'd you like me to show you around the place?

ANGELINA. That would be very nice.

(CECIL moves to her and takes her arm. They are just about to leave when Officer DOUGHBERG enters through the front door.)

DOUGHBERG *(to JOAN)*. Good morning, Sugar Duck.

JOAN *(puts a hand over her eyes)*. Oh, my—!

DOUGHBERG *(hurt)*. No? I stayed up half the night working on that one.

(On seeing the officer, Sister ANGELINA lowers her head. CECIL and PUG exchange looks.)

BEULAH. Officer Doughberg, you'll never guess what we just found out.

DOUGHBERG. Yeah? You'll never guess what I found out. *(He moves to ANGELINA.)*

BEULAH *(she indicates ANGELINA)*. This is the lady who raised Jimmy. Sister Angelina.

ANGELINA *(holds out a hand)*. Very nice to make your acquaintance.

DOUGHBERG. Thank you. *(He shakes her hand and then turns to BEULAH.)* Now, allow me to introduce you to someone. *(With his other hand he pulls off ANGELINA's cowl. The others react with shock and JOAN jumps to her feet.)*

JOAN. What're you doing?! *(She rushes over to Officer DOUGHBERG.)*

DOUGHBERG. This is NOT Sister Angelina, this is Angie Ledbetter, better known as Angle Angie! *(ANGELINA looks up and smiles sheepishly.)* Known con artist, her main scams include the old shell game and Three Card Monte.

(PUG starts off but CECIL grabs his arm.)

ANGELINA. Oops. *(She looks around.)* Anybody got a cigarette?

GRETCHEN *(moves to BEULAH)*. I KNEW it! I KNEW that joker would pull something like this! *(She points to CECIL.)*

HUNTER *(sourly)*. Oh, great! Now I have to go back to dealing with those three horrible— *(On hearing this, IMOGENE and ZELDA turn and look at him. He smiles and clears his throat.)*

CECIL. Mom, I can explain.

DOUGHBERG. I'll just bet you can.

JOAN *(to DOUGHBERG)*. How'd you find out about her?

DOUGHBERG. We got a tip; somebody phoned the stationhouse.

ANGELINA *(to BEULAH)*. Ma'am, I know you're a very nice lady; Cecil told me all about you. And I know this looks bad but it wasn't any of his doing. This was all my idea.

IMOGENE *(a finger in the air)*. I knew something like this would happen. There was a low fog in my driveway.

(The others turn to look at her for a beat, then continue the scene.)

ANGELINA. I mean the part about me posing as a nun, that was my idea. But the rest of it, what I told you, that was the truth. He DID just turn up one day and I couldn't risk giving him over to the cops, as they'd take me in as well. But I want you to know I told him from the start that as soon as he got his memory back I'd take him to his real family. *(She takes BEULAH's hand.)* Please. You must believe me.

CECIL. She's telling the truth, Mom.

GRETCHEN. But you went right along with her, now didn't you?! *(To BEULAH.)* That shows you the kind of person he is!

BEULAH *(smiles)*. I believe her.

GRETCHEN & IMOGENE. WHAT?!

DOUGHBERG. Very touching. *(He takes ANGELINA's arm.)* Let's go.

JOAN. But she hasn't broken any laws!

DOUGHBERG. What about fraud? Running a con game, there's several others I can come up with once I put my mind to it. *(He pulls ANGELINA toward the front door.)* Come on, get in the car.

ANGELINA. Shotgun.

DOUGHBERG. Don't get cute. *(To BEULAH.)* I'll make sure this one won't be bothering you anymore. *(To ANGELINA.)* You know the route, let's go. *(They move to the front door.)*

ANGELINA. Flip you to see who drives.

DOUGHBERG. Now what did I just say to you?

CECIL *(moves to BEULAH)*. Mom, this isn't her doing. She just thought that as a nun it would make it easier for you to believe her. *(He eyes GRETCHEN.)* Some people around here are hard to convince.

BEULAH. Officer Doughberg, you can release her.

DOUGHBERG. What?! But she tried to—

BEULAH *(moves to DOUGHBERG)*. I know what she tried to do but, if I understand the law correctly, she can't be arrested if I don't press charges. Is that right?

HUNTER. That's the law. *(He smiles.)*

DOUGHBERG. Yes, ma'am, but she—

BEULAH. Please. Let her go.

CECIL. Thank you, Mom.

DOUGHBERG. Shoot! *(He kicks the floor like a little boy.)* I NEVER get to collar anyone in this place! *(To ANGELINA.)* At least, I can see you off these premises.

ANGELINA *(arm out)*. You may take my arm.

DOUGHBERG. Get going. *(He grabs the door handle.)* What made you show dressed like a nun?

ANGELINA. I was going to come here pretending to be a cop but they told me you were doing that.

DOUGHBERG. Out!

ANGELINA *(waves)*. See you later, Cecil.

CECIL. Thanks, Angie.

(Smiling, ANGELINA exits out the door followed by Officer DOUGHBERG.)

GRETCHEN *(to BEULAH)*. Now do you see the kind of people that imposter has working for him!

BEULAH. But none of that has to do with him, can't you see that? All that has happened after she found him. I tell you, he's my Jimmy! *(The sisters stare at her in disbelief.)* Can't any of you SEE that?

GRETCHEN. We'll get to the bottom of this. And I mean today! Mother, I want you to talk to someone.

BEULAH. Who?

GRETCHEN. A psychiatrist.

BEULAH. What? What're you saying?

GRETCHEN. I put in a call to Phoebe Wallenstein and I just got a call from her secretary. She's coming over here today. In fact, she'll be here at eleven thirty.

BEULAH. Oh, this is just a lot of nonsense, I can prove... wait. Hunter! *(She moves to HUNTER and the two talk quietly.)*

ZELDA *(moves to GRETCHEN)*. She's coming over here? So soon?

IMOGENE. I thought you said she was very busy.

GRETCHEN. Oh, she's VERY busy but apparently she's dropping everything to take this case. *(Pompously.)* I suppose once she heard my name it must've carried a lot of weight with her.

HUNTER. I forgot all about that. I do still have it.

BEULAH. Go get it and bring it back here.

HUNTER *(rushes to the front door)*. I'm on it. *(He exits.)*

(GRETCHEN moves to BEULAH, followed by IMO-GENE and ZELDA.)

GRETCHEN. Now, Mother, if you'll just listen to reason—

BEULAH *(waves her hand)*. I won't hear a word about it. You'll see, you'll ALL see! *(She exits through the manager's door.)*

GRETCHEN. But, Mother! *(The door closes in her face.)*

ZELDA. You shouldn't push her like that!

IMOGENE. Now she's mad.

GRETCHEN. She'll listen to reason. We'll just explain that if she DOESN'T talk to the shrink it will look bad for her.

ZELDA *(almost to herself)*. And then she'll say that WE were the ones who called in the psychiatrist in the first place.

GRETCHEN. Oh, just keep quiet, you two! *(She opens the door.)* Now, Mother— *(She exits followed by her sisters.)*

PUG *(to CECIL)*. Now what?

CECIL *(thinking)*. Quiet.

PUG. Okay…Gretchen!

CECIL *(shoots him a look and then looks at JOAN)*. I guess you're back to hating me again, right?

JOAN *(looks at him thoughtfully and then moves to him)*. No.

CECIL *(surprised)*. Huh?

JOAN. You could've hightailed it out of here last night… but you didn't. You stayed. And I know you're just doing it to help Mrs. Beulah. *(She leans over and gives CECIL a peck on his cheek. The two look at each other for a slight pause. Then CECIL puts his arms around her and the two kiss, their arms wrapped around each other.)*

PUG. No, no, pretend I'm not here.

(At that inopportune moment, Office DOUGHBERG enters through the front door.)

DOUGHBERG. Well, you won't be bothered by her and hey, HEY, HEY!!! *(On hearing this, JOAN turns, sees the officer and breaks from CECIL.)* When I said get his fingerprints I didn't mean like that!

(LIGHTS black out.)

Scene Three

(It is now almost eleven thirty. BEULAH is sitting on the sofa next to PUG. PUG holds out a deck of cards.)

PUG. Now take one.
BEULAH. Okay.
PUG. Eight of hearts!
BEULAH *(wide-eyed)*. That's RIGHT! *(She hands the card back to PUG.)* How'd you DO that?
PUG. I cheated.
BEULAH. Oh! *(She smiles at PUG.)* Clever.

PUG. Lesson here, never play with a stranger who brings his own deck of cards or pool cue. Not a good sign. *(He shuffles the cards.)*

BEULAH. I must remember that. Will you show me that again? I'd like to try it out on Hunter.

PUG. I'm guessing he might know a few tricks of his own.

(At that moment, ZELDA enters through the front door.)

PUG *(con't)*. And speaking of sneaky—

BEULAH *(rises)*. Zelda.

ZELDA *(sheepishly)*. Mother.

BEULAH *(to PUG)*. Thank you for the lesson, Parnell. *(She looks at ZELDA.)* When your sisters get back tell them I'll be in my office.

ZELDA. I will. *(She moves to BEULAH.)* Mother, please believe me, this wasn't my idea. Gretchen said—

BEULAH. I KNOW what Gretchen said. *(She moves to the manager's door.)* Now if you'll excuse me. *(She exits through the door.)*

ZELDA *(turns to PUG)*. I think she's still mad.

PUG. Gee, I wonder why. *(He rises and pockets the deck of cards.)*

ZELDA. I hate it when people get mad. I mean, I always try to get along, you know?

PUG. Why're you telling me?

ZELDA. I don't know. Nobody else I can tell, I guess.

PUG. Meanwhile, those two sisters of yours treat you like dirt.

ZELDA. That's not true!

PUG. They boss you around, run your life and tell you to shut up every time you open your mouth.

ZELDA. Well, they let me do some things I like.

PUG. I bet. *(He moves to the L door.)*

ZELDA. They let me keep the dogs.

(PUG stops at the door, looks out and then turns to ZELDA.)

PUG. Dogs? *(He moves to her.)* You have dogs?

ZELDA. Well, I'm trying to get them adopted out. You see, sometimes when a person passes away, and some of them are pretty old, they have pets. Usually a dog. Well, nobody, none of the families ever want them so I take care of them.

PUG *(smiling)*. Really.

(At this moment, CECIL enters through the L door. He watches the two talking.)

ZELDA. Right now I've got a poodle and two Dobermans. I love dogs.

PUG. I know; ain't they wonderful?

ZELDA *(warming up to PUG)*. Yes, they are.

PUG. Think about it. A dog is loyal, forgiving and brave, three things that people usually have to talk themselves into.

ZELDA. So true, so true. And their eyes!

PUG. Oh, I KNOW. You can just look into those big eyes and…and… *(PUG and ZELDA are now staring into each other's eyes)* …they so big…and sometimes sad… and… *(CECIL clears his throat. PUG turns to him.)* Cecil! THERE you are. *(CECIL smiles at him.)*

ZELDA. Well, if you'll excuse me I'll just go and see if the others are here yet. *(She smiles at PUG and exits out the front door. PUG watches her leave.)*

CECIL *(moves to PUG)*. You know, you may be right. *(Kidding.)* Maybe we SHOULD take off now.

PUG. Huh? Wait a minute, why did you change your mind all of a sudden? I mean, here we've come this far and— *(He catches on and punches CECIL in the shoulder.)* Oh, STOP!

CECIL *(imitating PUG)*. You can just look into those eyes…and they're so BIG!

PUG. Okay, okay, I get it. What's our next move?

(At that moment GRETCHEN and IMOGENE enter through the front door, followed by ZELDA.)

CECIL. I'm sure they'll tell us.

GRETCHEN. You two, don't leave the premises.

CECIL *(to PUG)*. Didn't I tell you?

IMOGENE *(to ZELDA)*. Is Mother still here?

ZELDA *(nods)*. She said to tell you she's in her office.

GRETCHEN. Right. *(She moves to the office door, followed by her sisters. ZELDA looks over at PUG. He points to her and she gets a determined look on her face and stops halfway.)* Okay, now— *(She sees ZELDA in the middle of the room.)* Just WHAT do you think you're doing?

ZELDA *(meekly)*. Nothing! *(She quickly trots over to her sisters as PUG holds up his hand in disgust.)*

GRETCHEN. Now. We'll all keep our calm and just act as if this were another day.

IMOGENE. Did I tell you I saw an owl— *(She points outside.)*

GRETCHEN *(cutting her off)*. And none of that!

(At that moment, JOAN enters through the front door.)

JOAN. Sometimes he can be SO dense!

CECIL. Joan! *(He crosses to her. PUG sits on the sofa and, pulling out his deck of cards, begins playing solitaire.)*

JOAN *(points to him)*. If you add some endearing word with that like "Plum" or "Beet" I'll sock you.

CECIL *(hands up)*. Wouldn't think of it. You get it straightened out with your boy in blue?

JOAN. I guess. We agreed to see other people. *(She looks at CECIL.)* Well, one of us did.

IMOGENE. What do we do once the psychiatrist gets here?

GRETCHEN. Did you hear what I just said? Act as you normally would.

ZELDA. You mean with you barking orders at us?

GRETCHEN. Yes. NO!

IMOGENE. Well, Zelda has a point. That would be a normal day.

(GRETCHEN notices the others watching them. She looks back at her sisters.)

GRETCHEN. Keep your voices down! *(She moves DR and motions her sisters to join her.)* Over here.

(ZELDA and IMOGENE move to her. As IMOGENE passes PUG she stops and looks at him curiously.)

PUG *(look up)*. Want me to tell your future? *(He thumbs the deck loudly. IMOGENE thinks about it.)*

GRETCHEN. Imogene!

IMOGENE. Coming! *(She moves to GRETCHEN.)*

GRETCHEN *(quietly)*. Now. First of all I do NOT bark orders!

IMOGENE. Bark, yell, demand, it's all semantics.

ZELDA. And then you get mad when we don't do what you want us to do.

IMOGENE *(to ZELDA)*. When did you EVER disobey Gretchen?

ZELDA. Just awhile ago. Didn't you see me? We were supposed to follow her over, and I didn't.

IMOGENE. Oh, some defiance. What did your horoscope say today?

GRETCHEN *(exploding)*. That's EXACTLY what I asked you NOT to DO!

(Unseen by the three sisters, PHOEBE enters through the front door. As soon as she enters, her attention is drawn to the sisters.)

IMOGENE. You said I should ask naturally.

GRETCHEN. But WITHOUT all the hocus-pocus!

IMOGENE. Oh, and you don't call that barking?

GRETCHEN. NO! I was MAKING A POINT!

ZELDA. Sounded like barking to me.

JOAN *(quietly, to PHOEBE)*. May I help you?

PHOEBE. Yes, my name is Phoebe Wallenstein. Someone here needed the services of a psychiatrist?

GRETCHEN. Oh, so NOW, today of all days, you two are ganging up on me?!

IMOGENE. Zelda was just making a point. We're not supposed to do THAT now?!

GRETCHEN. And just WHEN did you EVER listen to Zelda?!

IMOGENE. And just WHEN did you ever listen to ME?!

PHOEBE. Oh dear. *(She pulls out a notepad and pen.)* Looks like I got here just in time!

GRETCHEN. You're supposed to do what I TELL you!

ZELDA. I'm sorry.

IMOGENE *(to ZELDA)*. Will you stop apologizing?!

ZELDA. Did I do that again? I'm sorry.

PHOEBE *(writing)*. Oh my.

IMOGENE. You did it again!

ZELDA. No kidding? I'm— *(She catches herself)* —my bad.

PHOEBE. Persecution complex, full blown.

GRETCHEN. Can't you two just keep quiet? Why am I the only one with a head on my shoulders?!

IMOGENE. You?

GRETCHEN. Who has to do all the thinking for this family? It's a good thing you two have me around; you'd be lost without me.

PHOEBE. Delusions of grandeur—

IMOGENE. Oh sure, one minute you're acting like Madame Chairman and the next you're a tyrant. *(GRETCHEN fumes.)*

PHOEBE. Dissassociative behavior, possible bipolar tendencies.

JOAN. Oh, wait. Miss Wallenstein, they're not who… *(She stops and thinks.)*

IMOGENE. Why do you ALWAYS think you're the only one who's right? And that we don't have anything to say on ANYthing?

ZELDA. Yeah. We have feelings, you know.

PHOEBE *(to JOAN)*. What were you going to say?

JOAN *(after a beat)*. Uh…nothing. *(She and CECIL try to hide their smiles.)*

IMOGENE. Listen, Gretchen, my horoscope told me to take today one step at a time. That, along with that owl I saw, means only that we are all doomed to fail if we charge ahead!

PHOEBE. Failure to face reality. *(She flips a page in her notepad.)* I may have to bring in help!

IMOGENE. It doesn't hurt to read all the signs, you know.

GRETCHEN. Not TODAY! Look, that psychiatrist is due here any minute. She'll be walking through that door— *(She turns to point at the front door and sees PHOEBE.)* Who're you?

(ZELDA and IMOGENE turn to see PHOEBE.)

PHOEBE *(writing furiously)*. Just a minute. *(She stops writing and moves to the sisters.)* Phoebe Wallenstein. And I got here just in time. *(She pockets her pad and pen and rubs her hands together.)* Now, who wants to go first?

IMOGENE. Well, I'm Imogene and—

GRETCHEN. Wait a minute. What do you mean, go first?

PHOEBE. I think I may be able to do something here but you cannot expect miracles. Now. Why don't we start with you?

GRETCHEN. Me?

PHOEBE. Oh, would you prefer to lie down? *(She indicates the sofa. On seeing this, PUG gathers up his cards, pockets the deck and moves behind the sofa.)*

ZELDA. Her? *(She laughs.)*

GRETCHEN. Shut up, you!

PHOEBE. Have you always behaved in such a manner, or do you hear voices?

IMOGENE. No, you don't understand.

GRETCHEN. I should say not! I was the one who called you in. And your patient is our mother, Beulah Meadows.

PHOEBE *(disappointed)*. What?! You can't be serious.

ZELDA *(looking off)*. She's always serious.

PHOEBE. I thought it was you three.

GRETCHEN. What?

IMOGENE. Why us?

PHOEBE. After what you went through just now you have to ask me THAT? Wow, it was all I could do to keep up. You ladies are like some psychotic buffet!

GRETCHEN. Never mind us, will you PLEASE just examine our mother. Zelda, will you ask Mother to come out here?

ZELDA. Of course. *(She starts to move but PHOEBE grabs her arm.)*

PHOEBE. Do you always feel obligated to do what she says?

PUG. That's what I asked her.

(GRETCHEN and IMOGENE shoot a nasty look at PUG. Unruffled he smiles broadly and waves to them.)

ZELDA. Well, she knows best. *(She moves to the manager's door and exits.)*

PHOEBE *(shaking her head)*. Classic lamb psychosis.

GRETCHEN. Listen, Mrs. Wallenstein, I want you to know that I appreciate very much you getting here so quickly. I know you must have many other cases pending.

PHOEBE. That's true but this one sounded so interesting. Eighty percent of my clients these days just want to lose weight. *(She reluctantly takes out her pad and pen again.)* You SURE you don't want to tell me about your problems?

IMOGENE. Why, are you writing a paper?

PHOEBE. Paper, nothing! If I had you three for a month I could write a book!

(JOAN bursts out with a laugh and quickly covers her mouth.)

GRETCHEN. None of that, you! *(To PHOEBE.)* Did your secretary give you the details?

PHOEBE. Just a few. Tell me in your OWN words.

GRETCHEN. My mother has taken some vagabond off the street— *(she spins PHOEBE to face CECIL)* —him, and has convinced herself that he's our lost brother and her son who disappeared when he was seven years old.

(At that moment, BEULAH enters through the manager's door, followed by ZELDA.)

IMOGENE. Here she comes.

GRETCHEN *(quietly, to PHOEBE)*. Careful now, she may be hostile.

BEULAH *(moves to PHOEBE)*. Good morning. So nice of you to pay us a visit. *(She holds out a hand.)*

(PHOEBE shakes her hand and looks over her shoulder at GRETCHEN.)

PHOEBE. Oh, she's absolutely vicious.

GRETCHEN. Just do what we hired you to do.

PHOEBE. Yes, Your Grace. *(To BEULAH.)* My name is Phoebe Wallenstein and I'm a licensed psychiatrist. Do you mind if I ask you a few questions?

BEULAH. Certainly not. *(She shoots a look at her daughters.)*

PHOEBE. Why don't we sit down? *(She indicates the sofa.)*

BEULAH. Whatever you think is best. *(She sits on the sofa.)*

PHOEBE *(to GRETCHEN)*. I may have to use a chair and a whip. *(To BEULAH.)* Shall we begin?

(PHOEBE sits in the chair next to the sofa. GRET-CHEN, IMOGENE and ZELDA group together and stand nearby.)

BEULAH. Would you like some refreshment?

PHOEBE. I'm fine. Just a couple of standard questions. Please, just answer them to the best of your ability.

BEULAH. I shall do my utmost.

PHOEBE *(smiles at her)*. Very kind of you. Are you nervous?

BEULAH. Not at all.

GRETCHEN. That CAN'T be good! Any SANE person would be nervous!

PHOEBE *(looks at GRETCHEN)*. Are you going to try to tell me MY business now?

GRETCHEN. Sorry.

IMOGENE. Now you're starting to sound like Zelda. *(GRETCHEN elbows her.)* Oof!

PHOEBE. Now. What's your name?

BEULAH. Beulah Meadows. Maiden name Boone.

PHOEBE *(writing)*. Your age?

BEULAH. Sixty-eight. *(She catches herself.)* No, wait.

GRETCHEN. Ah HA! *(She points at BEULAH.)* See?

BEULAH. I mean I'll BE sixty-eight my next birthday.

PHOEBE. Very good.

IMOGENE. Objection! You're expressing an opinion.

PHOEBE *(to IMOGENE)*. First of all, this isn't a court and I'm not a judge. And second, you asked me over here to EXPRESS AN OPINION! *(She tries to compose herself as she looks at BEULAH.)* Sorry.

GRETCHEN. We won't interrupt again. *(She shoots a dirty look at IMOGENE.)*

PHOEBE *(to BEULAH)*. In which country do you reside?

BEULAH. The United States of America. Proudly.

PHOEBE. And who was the second president of the United States?

BEULAH. John Adams. *(PHOEBE keeps writing.)* Father of John Quincy Adams, our sixth president. *(PHOEBE smiles at this.)*

PHOEBE. Thank you. That should just about do it. *(She closes her pad.)*

GRETCHEN *(moves to PHOEBE)*. What? That's IT? That's all you're going to ask?

PHOEBE. And that's pretty much what she would be asked during any hearings as well.

GRETCHEN. What about her delusion? *(She points to CECIL.)* What about HIM?

PHOEBE. Very well. *(To BEULAH.)* Who is that man standing over there?

BEULAH. He's my son, James. We call him Jimmy.

PHOEBE. Thank you. *(She rises.)* I'll send you my bill as soon as—

IMOGENE. But he ISN'T our brother!

PHOEBE. But your mother says he is. Now, if you can prove that he's NOT your brother, then we can enter that as an *idée fixe*.

IMOGENE. Oh jeez, we're back to those words again.

GRETCHEN. And, in your best psychiatric advice, just how can we do that?

PHOEBE. Obviously, you've thought of running a DNA test on him.

(This leaves the sisters thunderstruck. Obviously, they haven't thought of this. They stare at each other for a moment.)

GRETCHEN *(trying to recover)*. Obviously, but we thought, you know, those are so…so…

PHOEBE *(nodding)*. So expensive. Also they can take months sometimes.

GRETCHEN. Exactly.

IMOGENE. Any OTHER ways you might suggest?

PHOEBE *(thinking)*. Well, there MIGHT be a way.

GRETCHEN. What? Anything!

PHOEBE. I could hypnotize him.

CECIL. Huh?

PUG. Oh, THAT old scam.

PHOEBE. No, no. I'm a certified hypnotist. And I've had great success in the past. Of course, this may not stand up in court, but if something comes out...

CECIL *(moves to the others)*. But...what if I don't let you hypnotize me?

PHOEBE. Well, that might look like an admission of guilt. Circumstantial, I know—

(Everyone is looking at CECIL. He nervously tugs at his shirt collar.)

CECIL *(after a long pause)*. Okay. I'll do it. *(He moves to the sofa.)*

PUG. CECIL!

CECIL. There's no other way, Pug. *(He sits next to BEULAH.)* Besides, she may not be able to hypnotize me.

PHOEBE. We'll see. Mrs. Meadows, would you be so kind as to move from the couch? I need my subject to be in line with me with no one else near him.

BEULAH *(rises)*. Certainly. *(She moves to PUG.)*

PHOEBE. We don't wish to run the risk of someone else intercepting. *(She sits in the chair and takes out a pen.)*

IMOGENE. What good will that do, you hypnotizing him?

PHOEBE. Well, with luck, we can get him to regress back to his childhood. How old was he when he disappeared?

BEULAH. Seven. That's when he lost his memory.

PHOEBE. Fine. *(She looks at CECIL.)* Now. If you'll just look at this pen.

CECIL. Right.

PHOEBE. And may we have total silence in the room? *(She shoots a look at the sisters.)* If that's at ALL possible!

GRETCHEN. We'll be quiet.

PHOEBE. Will wonders never cease? *(To CECIL.)* Now just relax and let your eyes follow the pen.

CECIL. I'll do my best. *(He concentrates on the pen.)*

PHOEBE *(as she moves the pen).* There is nothing else in the room. Only the movement of this pen. Back and forth, back and forth...

CECIL *(eyes widen).* Yes...back and forth...

PHOEBE. Just relax...relax...

(At that inopportune moment, DOUGHBERG enters through the front door.)

DOUGHBERG *(loudly).* Okay, I'm here to have it out right now!

(The tension breaks as everyone turns to Officer DOUGHBERG.)

JOAN *(rushes to DOUGHBERG).* Oh, for heaven's sake, don't just burst into this room like that!

DOUGHBERG. Why, what do I have to lose?

JOAN. We'll talk later, okay? Right now we're in the middle of something. *(She moves over to the others.)*

DOUGHBERG. Oh, sure! *(He follows JOAN over.)* You have time for everybody else but me!

GRETCHEN. Will you SHUT UP!

DOUGHBERG *(meekly)*. Yes, ma'am, sorry.

PHOEBE *(to CECIL)*. Where were we?

PUG. Back and forth.

PHOEBE. Right, thank you. *(Back to CECIL.)* Just follow the pen. Relax…

CECIL *(again, with wide eyes)*. Relax…

PHOEBE. You're getting drowsy. Your eyelids are getting heavy.

CECIL. They…they're not…they… *(Slowly he closes his eyes.)*

PHOEBE. Can you hear me? Can you hear my voice? *(CECIL nods slowly.)* Fine. Now, what is your first name?

CECIL. Cecil.

PHOEBE. And why did you come here, to this particular location?

CECIL. I was…we were going to rob it.

(PUG shakes his head vigorously and starts to speak, but BEULAH holds up a finger to him.)

PHOEBE. You are a petty criminal, then?

CECIL. I…wouldn't say petty. I…we only take what we need.

PHOEBE. I see.

(GRETCHEN points to CECIL and looks at her mother.)

GRETCHEN *("See")*. Huh? *(BEULAH shushes her.)*

PHOEBE. And your name has always been Cecil. Is that true?

(CECIL starts to answer but stops as if thinking.)

DOUGHBERG *(blurting out)*. You mean this is working?!
PHOEBE *(to DOUGHBERG)*. PLEASE! *(She looks at CECIL whose eyes open.)* Wait! *(She holds up the pen again.)* Watch the pen. Concentrate on the pen. Back and forth... *(She moves the pen back and forth.)*
CECIL. Yes, back and forth... *(He closes his eyes again.)*
PHOEBE. Don't take your eyes off the pen. Concentrate. *(After a slight pause.)* Now, do you remember another name? As a child, were you ever called by another name? *(CECIL nods. Unseen by the others, Officer DOUGHBERG also nods.)* Back when you were a child? *(Again both CECIL and Officer DOUGHBERG nod.)* And what was that name?

(Before CECIL can speak, Officer DOUGHBERG speaks.)

DOUGHBERG. Pillsbury.

(The others, except for CECIL, look at him.)

JOAN *(turns to DOUGHBERG)*. Oh, for heaven's sake! *(She punches Officer DOUGHBERG in the arm, waking him.)*
DOUGHBERG. Huh? What?
PHOEBE. Will SOMEONE take him out of here?
JOAN *(grabs DOUGHBERG's arm)*. Let's go outside.

DOUGHBERG. What happened?

JOAN. We can talk out there. *(She pulls Officer DOUGH-BERG through the front door and closes it behind them.)*

PHOEBE. Now. *(She again turns to CECIL.)* You were called another name? What was that name?

CECIL. It was...it was...Ji...Jimmy!

PHOEBE. Jimmy. Very good.

GRETCHEN. Oh, MOTHER told him that.

PHOEBE. Quiet.

CECIL. Is that...is that my sister? My oldest sister?

PHOEBE. Yes. *(GRETCHEN throws her hands in the air.)* Can you tell me her name?

CECIL. It's Gretchen. *(IMOGENE and GRETCHEN exchange looks. CECIL then smiles.)* Gerty the Grump.

GRETCHEN. What?

ZELDA. Oh goodness, that's your old nickname!

CECIL. Was that Zee?

ZELDA *(amazed)*. Oh! Jimmy was the only one who EVER called me that!

IMOGENE. Mother could've told him that!

CECIL. And the Spook!

(IMOGENE's eyes widen and she quickly looks at CECIL.)

BEULAH. I didn't know THAT one!

IMOGENE. He couldn't know...I mean...how'd HE know that?

BEULAH. Ask him about the accident. How he lost his memory.

PHOEBE *(to CECIL)*. Now, go back in your mind. Remember. You are now seven years old. Just before you lost your memory, *(CECIL nods.)* Something happened then. What was it?

CECIL. I remember...I...I was flying. *(The others look at him in confusion.)* I was in the air. No, I was on a ride. It was a roller coaster!

PHOEBE. Yes. And then what happened?

CECIL. I was in the ride and something happened. I fell out of the ride, I...NO! I was PUSHED out of the ride.

GRETCHEN *(horror-struck)*. WHAT?!

BEULAH *(alarmed)*. Pushed! But the only other one in the car with him was... *(She shoots a look at GRETCHEN.)* Gretchen!

IMOGENE *(accusingly, to GRETCHEN)*. You PUSHED him?!

GRETCHEN. No, NO! It was only a nudge! *(She shoots a hand out as if shoving something. Catching herself, she pulls her arm back.)*

BEULAH *(moves to GRETCHEN)*. You NEVER told us THAT!

GRETCHEN. More of an insinuation. Hey, he was acting silly and— *(She realizes.)* NObody knew that except— he really IS Jimmy!

ZELDA *(exploding)*. You vicious old witch!

GRETCHEN. You can't talk to me like that!

ZELDA. Why, you going to push me out of a roller coaster, too?!

(ZELDA, IMOGENE and BEULAH move to GRET-CHEN.)

GRETCHEN *(backing up)*. It was an accident! I...I don't have to listen to this! *(She rushes out the double doors.)*

BEULAH. Come back here, young lady!

(BEULAH exits out the door after GRETCHEN, followed by IMOGENE and ZELDA. PHOEBE looks at the door and then at CECIL.)

PHOEBE. Well…it worked.

(CECIL comes "out" of it.)

CECIL. Great work, Marge!

(PHOEBE and CECIL rise and shake hands.)

PUG *(moves to the others)*. Wow, you even had ME believing it.

PHOEBE. What a blast! I really had 'em going, didn't I?

CECIL. You were perfect!

PUG. How'd you switch places with the real shrink?

PHOEBE. Simple. I called her secretary, posing as Gretchen, and canceled the appointment. Then I called here, acting as Wallenstein, and you know the rest.

CECIL. Where'd you get all that stuff, that "Gerty" and "Spook" stuff?

PHOEBE. Ah, some nimrod videotaped their last Christmas party and put it on YouTube. Say, where'd you get that bit that you were pushed? I didn't tell you that.

CECIL. You didn't? Oh, it just came to me. You know the old con, you throw the ball back into their court; make them play defense.

PUG. Well, you certainly hit pay dirt with that one.

(At that moment, JOAN enters through the front door.)

JOAN. Sorry about that. *(She sees the three talking.)* Wha'd I miss?

PHOEBE. All done. He's really THE James Meadows.

JOAN *(astounded)*. He IS!

PHOEBE *(hand up)*. On my honor as a practicing psychiatrist. Now, if you'll excuse me, I have other cases pending. *(She winks at CECIL, who smiles, and exits out the front door.)*

JOAN *(to CECIL)*. What did you DO?

CECIL *(wide-eyed)*. I don't remember.

(BEULAH enters through the double doors.)

BEULAH. Well, they'll certainly listen to me NOW!

JOAN. The hypnosis worked then?

BEULAH. Oh, I didn't need all that mumbo-jumbo to tell me what I already knew.

JOAN *(not sure)*. Right. *(She looks at CECIL.)*

BEULAH. However, we're not finished yet.

CECIL. Huh?

BEULAH. There's someone else who STILL doesn't believe.

JOAN. Oh, whatever you say, Mrs. Beulah, is just fine with me.

BEULAH. I don't mean you.

(At that moment, HUNTER enters through the front door.)

HUNTER. Sorry I'm so late. Took me awhile to find that thing.

BEULAH. You have it, then?

HUNTER *(pats his jacket pocket)*. Right here.

PUG. I'm missing something here.

CECIL. Me, too. Who ELSE doesn't believe I'm Jimmy?

BEULAH. You.

CECIL. What?

BEULAH. You STILL don't know, do you? Well, I fore-saw this happening. Hunter?

HUNTER *(pulls out a sealed envelope)*. Got it right here.

BEULAH. Years ago I thought you might come back and I wrote down a few thoughts.

HUNTER. And she gave it to me for safekeeping. *(He holds up the envelope.)*

BEULAH. This is proof.

CECIL. I don't see how—

BEULAH. Just wait. Hunter, if you'd be so kind?

HUNTER. First, the formalities. *(He shows the envelope to BEULAH.)* Is this the document you handed me years ago?

BEULAH. It is.

HUNTER *(opening the envelope)*. And you can see I am now breaking the seal. *(He pulls out the letter inside. He hands it to BEULAH.)*

BEULAH. No, go ahead and read it.

HUNTER. Certainly. *(He scans the letter and gets a strange look on his face.)* This is IT? THIS is your PROOF?

BEULAH. Go on.

HUNTER. Very well. *(He moves to CECIL, who eyes him curiously. HUNTER reads.)* "If it is true that a personality is formed by age three then some characteristics will ring true. *(He looks at CECIL.)* Ready?

CECIL. I guess. Go ahead.

HUNTER *(after a brief pause)*. Cheese Whiz.

CECIL *(laughs out loud)*. Aw, stop it; you know that always makes me… *(he realizes and spins around to BEULAH, who is now standing next to him)* …laugh! *(He becomes emotional.)* How'd…how'd you know that? I mean, I didn't…I… *(He looks at PUG who shakes his head vigorously. He looks back at BEULAH.)* But that means… *(BEULAH nods.)* You're…you really ARE… *(The two hug.)*

BEULAH *(fighting the tears)*. Hadn't I been telling you all along?

(PUG pulls out a handkerchief and blows his nose.)

JOAN *(moves to HUNTER)*. Is that what it says?

HUNTER. It says he'll laugh when he hears the phrase. *(He smiles at CECIL.)* And he did.

CECIL *(still looking at BEULAH)*. Yes, I did.

BEULAH. You remember when I gave you those sandwiches I said I was sorry I didn't have your favorite.

HUNTER. Of course, not to rain on your parade but you realize those daughters of Beulah's really ARE your sisters.

CECIL. Oh, right. *(He gets a disgruntled look on his face.)*

PUG. Hey, Zelda ain't all that bad. *(Beaming.)* She promised to show me her Dobermans.

HUNTER. Show you her WHAT?

CECIL. Now, Mother, if you'll excuse me. *(He moves to JOAN.)* I believe I have a lunch date.

JOAN. Hey, that's right. *(CECIL holds out his arm and JOAN takes it.)*

CECIL *(to BEULAH)*. Don't wait up for me…Mother. We MAY be a little late. *(He escorts JOAN to the front door.)*

BEULAH. Joan, you're going out with Jimmy now?

JOAN *(looking back, smiling)*. Yes, ma'am. *(She looks at CECIL.)* I lost a bet. *(They exit out the front door.)*

PUG *(leans in to BEULAH)*. You know? I think your boy has a girl.

BEULAH. You know? I think you're right. Say, I have a question.

PUG. Whazzat?

BEULAH. What's Three Card Monte?

PUG *(pulls out a deck of cards from his pocket)*. Ma'am, you came to the right man. Take a seat. *(BEULAH sits on the sofa and PUG sits next to her.)* The game is called Three Card Monte. Sometimes it's also called "Find the Lady" and in New Orleans it used to be called "Tossing the Broad." *(HUNTER stands behind them and smiles as he watches.)* First we need two aces and a queen. *(He pulls three cards off the top of the deck and shows them—two aces and a queen.)* Why, lookee there! What're the odds? *(As he places the cards facedown on the coffee table, the LIGHTS start to dim.)* And here we go. Here's the lady. *(He picks up the queen, shows it to BEULAH and replaces it facedown between the two aces.)* Keep your eye on the lady. *(He deftly moves the cards over and under one another. BEULAH and HUNTER try to watch the queen.)* Round and round she goes, where she stops, nobody knows. In and out and round about…

(LIGHTS black out.)

END